Trade Like Jesse Livermore

Trade Like Jesse Livermore

RICHARD SMITTEN

WILEY

John Wiley & Sons, Inc.

Published by John Wiley & Sons, Inc., Hoboken, New Jersey.
Published simultaneously in Canada.

For general information on our other products and services, or technical support, please contact our Customer Care Department within the United States at 800-762-2974, outside the United States at 317-572-3993 or fax 317-572-4002.

Wiley also publishes its books in a variety of electronic formats. Some content that appears in print may not be available in electronic books.

For more information about Wiley products, visit our web site at www.wiley.com.

Library of Congress Cataloging-in-Publication Data:

Smitten, Richard.
    Trade like Jesse Livermore / Richard Smitten.
        p.   cm.—(Wiley trading series)
    Includes index.
        ISBN 0-471-65585-6 (cloth)
    1. Investment analysis—Case studies.   2. Stockbrokers—United States.   3.
Livermore, Jesse L. (Jesse Lauriston) 1877–1940.   I. Title.   II. Series.
    HG4529 .S558   2005
    332.64'5—dc21   2004013490

0-471-65585-6

Printed in the United States of America.

10   9   8   7   6   5   4   3   2   1

Contents

Preface

Trade Like Jesse Livermore explains the complete Livermore Trading System, developed by Jesse Livermore over his legendary 45-year career trading the stock market. This book explores the technical aspects of the Livermore Trading System, including Timing, Money Management, and a way to achieve Emotional Control. It deals with the details and secrets of the stock trading system that brought about Livermore's amazing and unbridled success on Wall Street.

The information in this book comes as a result of over two years of deep research and many personal interviews with the remaining Livermore heirs. In 2001, I wrote the only complete biography of Jesse Livermore: *Jesse Livermore—World's Greatest Stock Trader*, published by John Wiley & Sons., Inc. This is a very personal memoir about the famous trader and covers every aspect of his life from the time he ran away from home in 1891 until he shot himself in 1940.

For that book, I was able to interview Paul Livermore, Jesse's son, who was a recluse and had never spoken to anyone about his father. Paul provided insights into his father's trading and his methods that had never been disclosed. Paul was 77 at the time and died shortly after these interviews.

I also interviewed Patricia Livermore, Livermore's daughter-in-law, married to Jesse Livermore Jr. She provided not only several personal anecdotes, but also some information about how Livermore prepared for his day of trading and how he prepared his mind to trade in the massive positions he often took.

Livermore made four separate fortunes and caught the crash of 1907 on the short side: He made over $3 million in a single day. In the Market Crash of 1929, he made over $100 million.

Livermore was not a fundamentalist in his trading approach—he was a true technical trader. He believed that the technical trading of stocks, recurring numerical and chart patterns are nothing more than the graphic reflection of such human emotional behavior as greed, fear, ignorance, and hope. Livermore knew how to recognize these recurring patterns and made several fortunes as a result of this knowledge. "Wall Street never changes," he said, "because human beings never change."

Through trading and market observation, Jesse Livermore found that stocks and stock markets move in cycles within a series of repetitive patterns. He then developed a set of unique tools, using mathematical formulas and equations that allowed him to identify and interpret the movement in stocks with uncanny reliability. His amazing trading record over the 45 years of his career made him one of the most famous traders to ever work on Wall Street. He is still regarded by many professional traders as the greatest trader who ever lived.

Livermore worked in total secrecy in a highly secure New York City penthouse at 780 Fifth Avenue, the Heckscher Building. He once wrote, "On October 5, 1923, in order to practice my new techniques and theories, I moved my offices to Fifth Avenue. I designed the offices very carefully. I wanted to be away from the Wall Street atmosphere, out of earshot of any tips. I also wanted to gain more secrecy in my operations and more security, so that no one could know my trades. Sometimes I used over fifty brokers to keep my trades secret."

It was here in these offices that Livermore applied his interpretive skills with the technical tools available to him at the time: board boys recording market movement on a chalkboard; telephone lines connected directly to the exchanges in New York, Chicago, London, and Paris; and a number of ticker tapes spitting out the most current stock and commodity quotes. He proved his trading system over and over again by taking advantage of the accurate price movements predicted by his trading system.

Under the pseudonym Larry Livingston, Jesse Livermore was the real protagonist in another best-selling book: *Reminiscences of a Stock Operator*, published in 1923 (also currently published by John Wiley & Sons). That book explained what he did, like cornering entire commodity markets such as cotton and coffee, and making $3 million in a single day by going short in the crash of 1907, but that book did not explain how he did it.

This book explains Livermore's trading methods, techniques, and technical formulas. It reveals the Jesse Livermore Trading System in complete detail. All of these trading methods can be applied to today's trading techniques, using personal computers and the Internet.

The book explains a number of aspects of Livermore's technical trading systems, such as:

- Recognizing and profiting from Pivotal Point Trading
- Continuation Pivotal Points and how to recognize them
- One- and three- day reversal signals—how to identify them and profit

- Tandem Trading—looking at two stocks, the stock and the sister stock
- Industry Group action and how it must be analyzed and understood before trading
- Top Down Trading techniques
- The importance of volume activity in trading a stock
- Stocks breaking out to new highs and what that can mean for a trader
- Break-outs from a consolidating base
- Trading only in the leading stocks in each group
- The dimension of time, an important element in trading the Livermore system
- The complete Livermore Money Management system

The Livermore Trading System can be applied to any trading time frame from 10 seconds to 10 years, and it can be used by the long-term trader as well as the day trader.

Like an athlete preparing for a contest, Livermore considered it very important to prepare himself both psychologically and physically for a day of trading. These techniques are disclosed in this book.

[NOTE: As a result of his Jesse Livermore research, Smitten currently is putting together a fully automated software program that allows the trader to trade like Jesse Livermore. This software program is the main asset of a company that was taken public and started trading on the Nasdaq Bulletin Board on April 1, 2003, under the symbol SMKT-Stock Market Solutions. This highly technical software program has led to an even deeper study of Livermore's trading methods and formulas. Much of this detailed technical material is included in this book.]

LIVERMORE TRADING SYSTEM— STRUCTURE OF THE BOOK

The Livermore system has three main headings: Timing, Money Management, and Emotional Control.

Timing—When to Pull the Trigger

Chapter 4 explores the technical tools Livermore used to determine when to pull the trigger and actually initiate the trade. This includes graphic studies using charts, tables, and examples of Pivotal Points, as well as how to recognize Continuation Pivotal Points and one- and three-day stock reversal patterns. The importance of high-volume breakouts are explained. Stocks breaking out to new highs are also demonstrated and explored in detail. All these factors are necessary to fully understand the Livermore Trading System.

The Livermore Money Management System

This is a system used by Livermore that explains to the trader "when to hold 'em and when to fold 'em." The five rules of Livermore's money management are explained in full detail in Chapter 5.

> Rule 1—Use a unique probe system.
> Rule 2—Never lose more than 10 percent on any trade.
> Rule 3—Always keep a cash reserve.
> Rule 4—Don't sell just because you have a profit; you need a reason to buy and to sell.
> Rule 5—After experiencing a windfall profit put half the profit in the bank.

Emotional Control

Chapter 6 discusses how to keep your emotions under control and follow the Livermore Trading System. Livermore believed emotional control to be perhaps the most difficult thing for a trader to master. Often, a successful trader has the biggest battles within himself, in following his own rules. Livermore's rules for emotional control are explained in detail in this book. A quick summary follows:

- Learn from your mistakes: Keep notes and analyze every trade.
- Preparation: Livermore had a daily regime, almost a trading ritual.
- His Special Office Arrangement: Keep strict office rules such as no talking after opening bell.
- Masterminding the media: Be suspicious of the news media—read between the lines.
- Cut losses/control emotions: A TRADER MUST LEARN AND PRACTICE EMOTIONAL CONTROL.
- Let the winners ride: Don't dump a winning trade.
- Follow your own rules.
- Beware of stock tips: Never take stock tips under any circumstances.

Livermore finally concluded—perhaps his most important observation—that emotional control is every trader's major challenge and is often the most important element in successful trading. He went so far as to take college courses in psychology to try and better understand the human mind. He considered faulty emotional control as his major trading flaw. He said to his sons, *"I only lost money when I did not follow my own rules."*

The book explains the importance of discipline in following the trading rules. It outlines how Livermore traded and how the reader can do so as well.

Each chapter of this book deals with one or more of Jesse Livermore's trading theories, methods, and techniques. In some cases, they have been updated to take advantage of the advanced technology that is currently available to today's technical traders. The book includes a large number of charts, graphs, and tables. It is designed for the trader who wants to become a master trader, like its subject.

Richard Smitten

Acknowledgments

I would like to thank my friend and partner Dennis Kranyak for all his hard work in helping me prepare this book. Dennis hand-built all the charts in the book and indexed, for the first time, all the famous Livermore quotes in Chapter 9.

Dennis has been with me on the Jesse Livermore journey for more than five years while we studied all the Livermore methods, trading techniques, and secret formulas. He has always kept it fun and interesting, and I am always astounded by his facile and brilliant mind.

Thanks, Dennis.

RICHARD SMITTEN

Trade Like Jesse Livermore

CHAPTER 1

Meet Jesse Livermore

J esse Livermore was perhaps the best stock trader who ever lived. During his lifetime, he was a legend of Wall Street. He was "The Boy Plunger," "The Wolf of Wall Street," "The Great Bear of Wall Street." When he was alive, he was as famous as Warren Buffett is today, although they had entirely different trading techniques.

He was a quiet and secretive man, given to keeping his own counsel. After losing several fortunes by listening to tips and the advice of men he thought were smarter than he was, he closed his offices near Wall Street at 111 Broadway, moved up to the Heckscher Building at 780 Fifth Avenue, and set up a palatial suite of offices. On one of his many trips to Europe, he had found a manor house in England with a huge paneled library. He bought the library, including books, paneling, and furniture. He had it disassembled in England and reconstructed in New York.

The library was highly secure, with a private keyed elevator. It occupied the entire penthouse floor. When visitors exited the elevator, they found themselves in front of a big metal door that opened onto a small anteroom where Harry Dache would be waiting. Dache was a six-foot-six, former merchant mariner. He was Livermore's bodyguard, chauffeur, confidante, and tutor of languages and life to his two sons. Once past Harry, visitors entered a suite of palatial offices, including one large room in which six men worked in silence on a walkway in front of a chalkboard, posting stock prices.

Once the market opened no one was allowed to talk. Livermore demanded silence for perfect concentration, so so that he could focus on the market and the price, time, and volume signals of the stocks he was inter-

1

ested in. With the ticker tape clicking, the chalkboard men posting the prices, and direct phone lines to the various stock exchange floors, the steady stream of current information never ceased after the opening bell. Livermore considered himself a student of the stock market all his life, and he loved it.

Livermore was born on July 26, 1877, in Shrewsbury, Massachusetts. His parents were New England farmers trying to scratch out a living from the rockstrewn fields. As a youth, Livermore was slight and sickly, which resulted in a lot of reading and solitude. He was a boy with a quick mind and good imagination, as well as a natural aptitude for numbers.

In a short while, he decided that his boyhood dreams and the adventures he had read about could not be realized in the unyielding New England countryside. At the age of fourteen, he was pulled from school by his father and sent to work in the fields. This only strengthened his belief that success rested in using his brain, not his body. He soon entered into a conspiracy with his mother, who supplied him with $5, and he formulated an escape plan. One afternoon, he simply slipped out of the farmhouse to the main road to Boston, hailed a wagon, and rode into the city. By chance, the wagon stopped in front of a Paine Webber brokerage office, and he wandered inside.

It was love at first sight for Livermore. He was enthralled with the brokers' office, city life, adventure, unbridled youth, and freedom. Paine Webber needed a chalkboard boy to post the stock prices for the customers, and he jumped at the opportunity. As far as Livermore was concerned, fate had extended a hand, and he grabbed it. Within hours of leaving the farm, he had a job, and with his meager funds he rented a room and became his own man before he was fifteen.

His mathematical brain set to work immediately as the quotes were yelled out by the customers from the ticker tape spitting out an endless stream. Soon, Livermore would challenge the crowd to yell out the quotes faster. With his brain in high gear and his concentration focused, he could write the numbers down on the board faster than the crowd could yell them. He felt alive with the challenge.

But Livermore was not just writing down numbers, he was in sync with them, in harmony, and soon he began to see recurring patterns and cycling trends. He kept a notebook, and during his breaks he would copy down these numbers to see if he could recognize the patterns.

He was also sensitive to the crowd. As the numbers changed and as the stocks moved up and down, so too did the mood of the crowd. They saw a stock's volume increase, and the excitement level increased. He could almost feel their heartbeats accelerate. He saw their eyes light up as their trading increased. It did not take him long to figure out that as they saw opportunities to make money their personalities changed. All of a sudden, there was an excitement in the air as the price climbed. But this excitement often died as the stock price rolled over and fell—the crowd became quiet, often sullen, and sometimes despondent.

Livermore was eventually able to define these emotions as greed and fear, the two dominant emotions that, he understood, drove market action. He noticed how the traders all talked among themselves, buoying their confidence, reassuring themselves; he also noticed how often they were wrong.

One day, the office manager told him something that he was to wrestle with for the early part of his life. "Hey, Kid, see how these guys all talk among themselves, figuring stuff out about why this happens and why that happens? You see how often they are wrong? Well, I'll tell you something that could help you: It isn't what these guys say to each other that counts—it's only what the goddamn tape says that counts!"

At first, Livermore did not get it. But then one day the light went off in his brain: "Don't concern yourself with *why* things are happening, only observe *what* is happening. The reasons why will be eventually revealed to you—by then it will be too late to make money—the move will be over!"

Livermore was a good-looking, easygoing kid, with a quick smile and a calm demeanor. His keen intelligence and natural curiosity were obvious to those who knew him. Blond with a perfect set of white teeth, he stood five feet eleven inches tall. He always wanted to be six feet, and later in his life he owned 30 pairs of elevator shoes that raised him the extra inch he wanted. He always found ways to get what he wanted—it was a life pattern for him.

Livermore soon felt that he was receiving more than a university education, a specialty education in stock market trading. He made a series of observations in his diary that later helped make him millions. But he never was motivated only by money. Rather, he was motivated by curiosity, excellence, and a desire to be the best—the best stock trader who ever lived. He knew that the money would come. The money was the reward. Livermore made two observations at his young age:

1. The majority of traders and investors lost money on a consistent basis.
2. The majority of traders had no intelligent and consistent plan to trade the market. In effect they were gambling. Playing tips. Playing hunches. Playing the favorites of the moment. Playing all kinds of tips—tips from analysts, friends, insiders.

In other words, as far as Livermore was concerned, what he saw other traders doing was simply random-action stock picking—deadly and dangerous. The same is just as true in today's trading environment.

It was then that he decided to spend his life developing his methods, his strategy, and his stock-picking system. He did this in secret, for his own use. He was insatiable in his quest for knowledge. One of the clients in the brokerage house was a professor who, one day, gave him a book on the laws of physics, with the comment, "Maybe there is something in here that you can apply to the market."

There was. The professor had underlined. "A body in motion tends to stay in motion until a force or obstacle stops or changes that motion." Livermore thought long and hard about this, and agreed that *momentum* was a key factor in the behavior of stocks in both directions—*up* or *down*.

He kept his trading diary in secret. He was secretive and quiet by nature, feeling no desire to share his thoughts with others. He was like this all his life. He believed idle chatter was a waste of time and that all that really counted was action. And to him that was what the stock market was, pure action—every minute was dynamic and true: pure to itself and its own rules.

One day his boss caught him making entries into his secret diary. "Hey, Kid, you trading in your head making *pretend bets*? Useless waste of time, Kid. You gotta lay your money on the line in this game. Then you'll see that everything changes for you because your emotions take over, not your intellect. Don't waste your time with that pretend stuff."

Livermore discovered that his boss was correct. The minute the money goes on the line, everything changes. Even his physiology changed. His blood pressure increased, sweat appeared on his brow, he could feel his heart beat increase—the trade loomed as the largest thought in his mind. Yes indeed, his boss was correct, but Livermore liked the rush; it made him feel very alive.

When he was 15, six months after he had started at Paine Webber, he made his first trade. One of the other boys came to him and suggested they go across the street to the bucket shop.

Livermore agreed. He had some confidence in the recurring patterns he had noted in his diaries, and he had developed some trading methods in his mind and tested them on paper. He decided it was time to make his first real trade.

A bucket shop was a place where one could play the market on 10 percent margin. Its atmosphere was more like an offtrack betting parlor than a broker's office. The stock ticker spewed out the trades as they happened on the exchange, and the prices were recorded on the chalkboard. The rules were simple: Put up your 10 percent in cash, place a bet by buying a stock and receive a printed receipt for your purchase. Then sit back and watch the action. As soon as you lost 10 percent of the value of the stock, the house swooped in and took your money. Conversely, if the stock went up you could cash in your ticket at will. The house won almost all of the time. It was usually a sucker play—with the customers being the suckers. They were simply bad stock pickers.

The bucket shop kept the money. It was never used to buy the stock. The actual purchase of the stock was *booked* by the bucket shop, as bookies still do. Together, Livermore and his friend scraped together $10 to buy steel. Checking the calculations in his diaries, Livermore saw a good opportunity, and they placed their order. Within seconds, steel rose, and they closed out their trade with a profit of over $3 on a $10 play—Livermore was hooked. He had made in seconds what it usually took him a week to earn at his job.

Soon, Livermore quit his job and was playing the bucket shops. In a year, he amassed profits of over $1000. He returned triumphant to his parents' farmhouse and gave his mother back the $5 she had given him and $300 more, as a present. The visit showed them that at the age of 16 he had already become a successful stock market trader. His dumbfounded father accepted the money.

Livermore returned to Boston and continued his trading. As he did, he carefully recorded all his trades, studying them for patterns and trying to improve his methods. As time went by, he became so successful that he eventually was banned from every bucket shop in America.

Unable to play in the bucket shops, Livermore traveled to New York City. At 20 years of age, he arrived in New York with $2500 in his pocket. His stake had been as high as $10,000, but he had suffered reversals like everyone else. His philosophy, all his life, was simple: "Learn from your mistakes, analyze them. The trick is not to repeat your mistakes," which meant to Livermore you had to first understand your mistakes—find out what went wrong with the trade, and don't repeat the same mistake again.

Livermore considered his days trading the bucket shops as his education, his college days, his apprenticeship. He had already established some early rules. But could he follow them?

The first two trading rules Livermore had listed in his secret diaries: "Basic Rule:—Before pulling the trigger on a trade place as many factors in your favor as possible." Livermore felt that success was achieved when *all* the basic factors were in his favor, and he concluded that the more factors he could think of the more successful he would be.

The next rule was this: "No trader can or should play the market all the time. There will be many times when you should be out of the market, sitting in cash waiting patiently for the perfect trade."

So, armed with $2500 and his experience in the bucket shops, Livermore entered the action on Wall Street. He befriended E. F. Hutton and opened an account at his brokerage firm.

He began trading and almost immediately went broke. Then he had to figure out why.

He went to his friend and mentor E. F. Hutton for help.

Excerpt from *Jesse Livermore—World's Greatest Stock Trader* by Richard Smitten (John Wiley & Sons, 2001).

"Ed, I can't beat Wall Street right now. I'm going back to the bucket shops. I need a stake, then I'll be back."

"I don't get it." Hutton said. "You can beat the bucket shops, but you can't beat Wall Street. Why's that?"

"First off, when I buy or sell a stock in a bucket shop I do it off the tape; when I do it with your firm it's ancient history by the time my order hits the floor. If I buy it at say, 105 and the order gets filled at 107 or 108, I've lost the comfort margin and most of my play. In the bucket shop if I buy it off the tape I immediately get the 105. The same is true when I want to sell short, especially on an active stock where the trading is heavy. In the bucket shop I put my sell order in at say, 110, and it gets filled at 110, but here it might get filled at 108. So I'm getting it from both sides."

"But we give you better margin than the bucket shops." Hutton said.

"And that Ed, is what really killed me. With the extra margin from you I could stay with a losing stock longer, not like the bucket shop where a 10 percent move wiped me out. See, the point is that I wanted the stock to, let's say, go up and it goes down. Holding on to it longer is bad for a trader like me because I was betting it would go up. I can afford to lose the 10 percent but I can't afford a 25 percent loss on margin—I have to make too much back to get my money back.

"So, all you could ever lose in the bucket shops was the 10 percent because they would sell you out."

"Yes, and it turns out that was a blessing—all I ever want to lose in any one stock is ten percent." Livermore said. "Now, will you lend me the money?"

"One more question." Hutton smiled. He liked this boy—he was a force to be reckoned with, a mental force. "Why do you think you can come back here next time and win, beat the market?"

"Because I will have a new trading system by then. I consider this part of my education."

"How much did you come here with, Jesse?"

"Twenty-five hundred dollars."

"And you leave with a borrowed thousand dollars." Hutton said, reaching into his wallet and extracting the thousand in cash, handing it to Livermore. "Hell, for 3500 dollars you could have gone to Harvard."

"I'll make a lot more money with my education here than I ever would have, going to Harvard." Livermore said, smiling, as he took the money.

"Somehow, I believe you, Jesse."

"I'll pay this back." Livermore said, pocketing the money.

"I know you will. Just remember when you come back—do your trading here—we like your business."

"Yes sir, that I will." Livermore said.

Ed Hutton watched him leave. There was no question in his mind that he would see him again.

Jesse Livermore made and lost fortunes a number of times. He lived in opulence, maintaining several palatial homes complete with staff, including a permanent barber. He owned a yacht, and he and his wife kept his and her Rolls Royces. He even had a private railcar, which transported him to Chicago and the grain pits at the Board of Trade, although he never appeared on the floor of any exchange.

Livermore went bankrupt four different times; each time, he paid back every cent to his creditors when he got back on his feet. His skill in trading the market and the resulting incredible lifestyle did not, however, insulate him from tragic events, culminating in his suicide in New York's Sherry Netherlands Hotel in 1940.

Jesse Livermore was, and still is, considered by many Wall Street traders as The Greatest Trader Who Ever Lived. But The Greatest Trader Who Ever Lived knew that happiness was elusive and had nothing to do with wealth.

CHAPTER 2

Timing Is Everything

L ike the old real estate adage that everything is location, location, location, in trading the stock market it is timing, timing, timing. In order to assure himself that his timing was correct Jesse Livermore went through a complex checklist before he pulled the trigger on a trade. It was also his observation that on many occasions the timing on selling a stock was just as crucial as buying a stock; in fact, sometimes the selling was the more difficult decision. *Selling Harder*

Any stock trader will tell you that stock buying is the easier of the two trades—getting in is the fun part. When traders buy stocks they are full of hope and perhaps a touch of greed, so when they pull the trigger and buy a stock there is often a feeling of elation, euphoria, similar to the feeling a person gets when he makes a major purchase such as a car, or a house, or a boat. These feelings stem from the emotions of hope and greed. It is later, if the trade shows losses that these emotions often turn into fear. The trader has to fight a constant emotional battle.

This is where the second phase of Livermore's Trading System, the Money Management phase, becomes essential—choosing the moment to sell. Even if the stock goes in the right direction and the trader prospers by gaining several points, he still has to decide when to sell his position: Should I take the profit now, or should I wait?

The Livermore philosophy on this point is simple, like the rest of his trading strategies. You need valid reasons to buy, and you need valid reasons to sell. Some of Livermore's greatest long-term triumphs in the market occurred when he bought a stock and waited for a valid signal to sell. *valid reason to sell*

9

This book explains in detail when the *buy* signals occur and when the *sell* signals appear. It will be up to the astute trader to follow these signals correctly.

Your timing should never be dictated by high prices. High prices were never a timing signal to sell a stock. Just because a stock is now selling at a high price does not mean it won't go higher. Livermore was just as comfortable on the short side, if that was the direction of the trend. Just because a stock has fallen in price does not mean that it won't go lower. Livermore said: "I never buy a stock on declines, and I never short a stock on rallies."

Buying stocks as they made new highs and selling short as they made new lows was a contrarian point of view in Livermore's day. He let the market tell him what to do. He got his clues and his cues from what the market told him. He did not anticipate; he followed the message he received from the tape. Some stocks keep making new high or lows for a very long time, and therefore can be held for a very long time.

Livermore had a reputation as a high-flying speculator, not unlike a high-stakes gambler. Nothing could have been further from the truth. Livermore was more conservative in his trading than anyone ever knew. The Livermore Trading System was a disciplined procedure for him. Simply stated, it was an attempt to place as many factors in the trader's favor as possible. Or, put a different way, *don't make a trade until all the odds are in your favor.*

The trick for Livermore was to have the discipline to often *refrain* from trading until the perfect, or as close to perfect as possible, trade came along. And they did. Like streetcars, another one always came along—better to miss one than to get on the wrong car and take a trip to financial hell.

With this in mind, the first thing Livermore did in his timing system was to check the overall direction of the market. It is important to reiterate that he did not care which direction the market was moving. There was always a trade possible for him, either up or down, short or long. He always wanted the wind at his back. He wanted to trade with the trend, not against it. This may sound simple but just consider how many sophisticated mutual funds and investors were buying stock during the last few years when they should have been out of the market altogether, or selling short!

Figures 2.1–2.3 illustrate the dramatic fall the stock markets experienced over the last three years. They had been in decline long before the 9/11 tragedy and bottomed out soon after that date. The only way traders could make money in such a market was to trade the short side.

Figure 2.1 This chart (one of three) illustrates the precipitous fall the market has recently experienced.

This is usually prohibited for most mutual funds, which eliminated these type of funds from the possibility of making a profit under these circumstances.

Few people understand the short side of the market. In Livermore's day, as in the climate of today's trading, very few people would speculate on a stock going down. In fact, very few people understand that you can actually place an order to *short* a stock and make money as the stock price declines. Less than 4 percent of investors or traders actually ever short stocks.

Livermore shorted stocks, and this was one of several specific reasons why he was such a successful trader. He had concluded that the stock market goes up approximately a third of the time, sideways a third of the time, and down a third of the time. Therefore, if a trader only trades in anticipation of a stock rising in price he is wrong on the trade two thirds of the time!

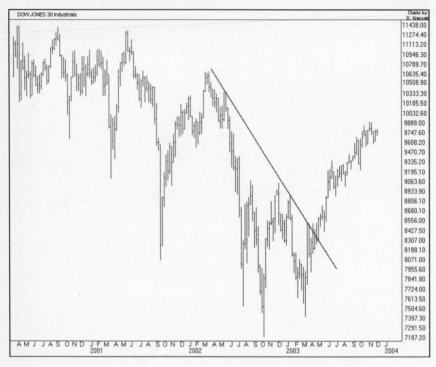

Figure 2.2   This chart (two of three) illustrates the precipitous fall the market has recently experienced.

The speculator Louis Smitten defines the steps of a short sale as follows: the sale of stock you don't own, in anticipation of a drop in price.

1. Stock is borrowed from your broker for delivery to your account.
2. Later, you purchase stock in the open market and return it to your broker to pay back the stock you borrowed. This completes the transaction.

In other words, the stock is sold first, then bought back at a later date, and at, it is hoped, a lower price. This is the reverse of a normal buy-first, sell-later transaction.

So, the first step in the Livermore procedure before making a trade is to determine the direction of the overall market—Livermore referred to

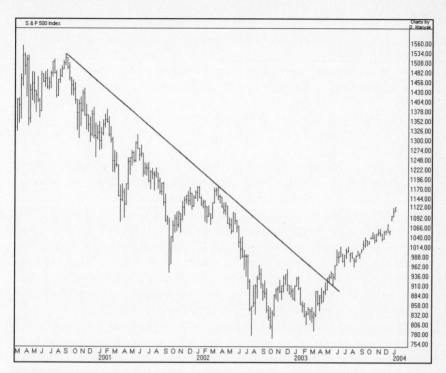

Figure 2.3 This chart (three of three) illustrates the precipitous fall the market has recently experienced.

this as *determining the Line of Least Resistance*. He did not generally use the terms "bull" or "bear" for a very specific reason: He felt these terms led the trader to have a mind set that would cause him to anticipate the direction of a trade or the direction of the market—a deadly and dangerous thing to do—because the market is a dynamic entity driven by people's emotions—not reason.

> *Don't try and anticipate what the market will do next—simply go with the evidence of what the market is telling you—presenting to you.*
>
> —Jesse Livermore

This is a complex, confusing area for traders in understanding the Livermore theory. There are times when his approach may appear contradictory and confusing. You may ask yourself: Isn't Livermore's whole theory a way of anticipating the direction of the market before it happens?

In the Livermore Trading System, the answers are always apparent in the actual performance of the stock. It is the trader's job to investigate the facts and solve the mystery, to be like Sherlock Holmes—only deal in the facts that are presented by the stock—*Do not anticipate what will happen next—Always wait for the market to confirm your trade.*

The successful speculator must formulate his plan in advance of a stock's movement. Because the market is driven not by logic but by emotion, it is most often unpredictable and goes against logic. Livermore believed that to even out the odds and increase the safety of a trade the trader had to wait for the market to confirm his judgment. This required patience and discipline, two rare traits in most people. But if you follow this advice, you are in effect getting insurance on your position because you have waited until the market has shown you what it is going to do. The rule is not to place your trade until the market itself confirms your opinion or shows you a different path to follow.

News items can often be deceiving. They can have less of an effect on the market than one might think or, by contrast, they can have a greater effect. The point is that there is no telling what effect news will have. As can be seen by the previous charts (Figures 2.1, 2.2, and 2.3), after the tragedy of 9/11 the market went down, but not as deeply or for as long as had been predicted. This was because the market had already been declining for more than a year.

It is too difficult to know what is going on in the inner workings of the market at the time of a news release. To illustrate: Perhaps the market has been in a long-term period with plenty of solid momentum behind it. In that case, a bullish or bearish piece of news may have no effect. The market also may be in an overbought or oversold condition and absorb the news item without a tremor, effectively "ignoring" the news.

When dealing with the news and its impact on the stock market, do not anticipate by using your own judgement and in effect "guess" what will happen. You must study the action of the market itself. As Livermore said: "Markets are never wrong—opinions often are. He also remarked:

Timing in the stock market is the key to success. A trader may deduce that a stock is going to go up or down in a big way and eventually he may be correct. In fact, if you have any experience in the market this will ring true. I knew that stock was going to go up ten points—I was just too darn early on the trade. I lost my money but I was ultimately right on the stock. I just moved too soon, the market went against me and I sold out my position for a loss. I even made a second attempt to buy it and it dropped three points, I got nervous, so I sold it.

Often a trader will move too soon and then doubt his opinion on the stock and sell it out. Or perhaps he makes other commitments and has no money left to buy the stock when it does make a move. Having been too hasty and having made two erroneous commitments, he loses courage. This is a common lament of stock traders.

What a trader is battling here is basically his greed. He wants every point out of the move and will kick himself if he is a point or two on the late side of the trade. Don't be anxious to make the trade. Wait for the confirmation of the market before you place your order. Think of it as a small insurance plan—lose a point or two and help eliminate the bad trades on the times when you are wrong and everyone is wrong on at least some of their trades.

Say, for instance, a stock is selling around $25 and has been consolidating within a range of $22 to $28 for a considerable period. Assuming that you believe that the stock should eventually sell at $50, have patience and wait until the stock becomes active, until it makes a new high, at around $28 to $29. Watch for an increase in volume activity, say 50% or more over normal volume. You will then know that you are correct. The stock must have gone into a very strong position, or it would not have broken out. Having done so, it is altogether likely that it is starting a very definite advance—the move is on. That is the time for you to back your opinion. Don't let the fact that you did not buy at $25 cause you any aggravation. The chances are if you had, you would have become tired of waiting and would have been out of it when the move started, because having once gotten out at a lower price, you would have become upset and perhaps fearful, and would not have gone back in when you should have.

A key factor in the Livermore Trading System's timing approach is to be correct in the trade right from the beginning. You should have waited patiently until all the factors were in place before pulling the trading trigger...therefore the stock should move in the direction of your trade almost simultaneously with entering the trade . . . that is, if you have acted correctly and been patient.

By contrast, if you have made a decision to enter a trade and the stock does not move quickly, and perhaps just lies there, languishing going sideways, or if it moves against you in the opposite direction of your trade, you should consider immediately closing out that trade.

Experience proved to Livermore that the real money made in speculating was "in commitments in a stock or commodity and showing a profit right from the start."

Livermore believed that if he was right in his timing and pulled the trading trigger at the appropriate moment, then the momentum would be like a tidal wave right behind the trade, and it had to go up. Therefore, if the stock did not go up right away he would have to assume his judgement was wrong. Yet there were times when Livermore admitted he did not have the patience to wait for the right moment, because he wanted to constantly be in the market.

You may well ask: With all his experience, why did he allow himself to break this rule? Livermore's answer: He was human and subject to human weakness. Like all speculators, he permitted impatience to outmaneuver good judgment.

There are aspects of trading that are very close to gambling, such as playing card games like poker and high-stakes bridge, which Livermore did every Monday night in his mansion on Long Island. Everyone who enjoys these games has an inclination to play every hand and win every pot. It is a key finger on the hand of greed, and if not curtailed by the self-discipline to adhere to the trader's own rules, it will almost surely become his greatest flaw. If not understood, it will surely bring about his downfall. Livermore exhorts the trader to have patience and wait until all factors are in his favor.

Livermore spent a great deal of time trying to determine when to sell a stock. The timing on the sale of a stock is just as important as the purchase. Your buy can be perfect, but unless you sell at the right time, the entire trade may not show a profit.

It is a human trait to be hopeful, especially when you buy a stock; and to be equally fearful when you sell. Livermore believed that when you inject hope and fear into the business of speculation, you face a very formidable hazard, because you are apt to get the two confused and in reverse positions.

Here is an illustration of the timing sequence in a typical trade. You buy a stock at $30.00. The next day it has a quick run-up to $32.00 or $32.50. You immediately become fearful that if you don't take the profit, you may see it fade away—so you sell and exit the trade with a small profit, at the very time when you should entertain all the hope in the world. Why should you worry about losing two points' profit that you did not have the previous day? If you can make two points' profit in one day, you might make two or three the next day, and perhaps five more the next week.

As long as a stock is acting right, and the market is right, be in no hurry to take a profit. You know you are right, because if you were not, you would have no profit at all. At this point, you should let the stock ride, and ride along with it. It may make a very large profit. As long as the market action does not give you any cause to worry, have the courage of your convictions . . . stay with it.

By contrast, suppose you buy a stock at $30.00, and the next day it goes to $28.00, showing a two-point loss. You would not be fearful that the next day would possibly see a three-point loss or more. No, most traders would regard it merely as a temporary reaction, feeling certain that the next day it would recover its loss. But that is the very time when you should be worried. That two-point loss could be followed by two points the next day, or possibly five or ten within the next week or two. That is when you should be fearful that, because you did not get out, you might be forced to take a much greater loss later on. That is the time you should protect yourself by selling your stock before the loss assumes larger proportions.

Livermore learned that *profits always take care of themselves but losses never do.*

His doctrine for the trader was to insure himself against considerable losses by taking the first small loss. In so doing, the trader keeps his account in cash so that at some future time, when a good trade presents itself, he will be in a position to go into another deal, taking on basically the same amount of stock as he had when he was wrong.

This strategy allows the trader to be his own insurance broker, because the only way he can continue trading stocks is to guard his capital account and never permit himself to lose enough to jeopardize his overall operations and be unable to trade at some future date, when his market judgment is correct.

Livermore was convinced that nothing new ever occurs in the business of securities or commodities trading or investing. There are times to speculate, and just as surely there are times not to speculate and stay out of the market.

He believed in a very true adage: *You can beat a horse race, but you can't beat the races.* This is true with the stock market. There are times when money can be made investing and speculating in stocks, but money cannot consistently be made by constant trading every day or every week of the year. Only the foolish will try. He felt that this strategy just was not in the cards and could not be done.

The trader may ask himself a major timing question: Why can't I just pick the correct time to buy a stock and then just forget about selling that stock because I am in for the long haul? If the last three years has taught us anything, it should be that there are no stocks that can just simply be bought and put away, hidden in our mattresses for the years to come.

Livermore believed that *there are no good stocks! There are only stocks that make money!*

This book offers some of Jesse Livermore's dos and don'ts for traders. One of the primary don'ts is: One should never permit speculative ventures to run into investments. Don't become an Involuntary Investor. Investors often take tremendous losses for no other reason than that their stocks are bought and paid for. How often have we all heard an investor say: "I don't have to worry about fluctuations or margin calls. I never speculate in the market. When I buy stocks, I buy them for an investment, and if they go down, eventually they will come back."

But unhappily for such investors, many stocks bought at a time when they were deemed good investments have later met with drastically changed conditions. These such so-called investment stocks frequently become purely speculative. Some go out of existence altogether. The original investment evaporates into thin air along with the investor's capital. This is due to the failure to realize that so-called investments may be called upon in the future to face a new set of conditions that would jeopardize the earning capacity of the stock, which was originally bought for a permanent investment.

By the time the investor learns of this changed situation, the value of his investment has most likely already greatly depreciated. The stock market moves in future time, not present time. Therefore, the so-called investor must guard his capital account, just as the successful trader does in his speculative ventures. Then, those who like to call themselves investors will not be forced to become unwilling investors—nor will trust fund accounts and mutual funds accounts depreciate so much in their value.

In Livermore's time it was considered safer to invest money in railroad stocks such as the New York, New Haven & Hartford Railroad than to have it in a bank. On April 28, 1902, New Haven was selling at $255 a share. In December of 1906, Chicago, Milwaukee & St. Paul sold at $199.62. In January of that same year, Chicago Northwestern sold at $240 a share. Look at those safe investments approximately 40 years later.

On January 2, 1940, they were quoted at the following prices: New York, New Haven & Hartford Railroad $.50 per share; Chicago Northwestern at 5/16, which is about $0.31 per share. On January 2, 1940, there was no quotation for Chicago, Milwaukee & St. Paul, but on January 5, 1940, it was quoted at $.25 per share. In Livermore's time, hundreds of stocks considered gilt-edged investments eventually were worth little or nothing. Great investments tumble, and with them the fortunes of so-called conservative investors in the continuous distribution of wealth.

There is no question that stock market traders have lost money. But Livermore believed that the money lost in the long run was small compared to the gigantic sums lost by so-called investors who have let their investments ride. The same is true in the current 1999–2004 stock market, as illustrated in the market charts at the end of this chapter. From Livermore's viewpoint, the investors are the big gamblers. They make a bet, stay with it, and if it goes wrong, they lose it all. The trader might buy at the same time. But if he is an intelligent trader, he will recognize—if he keeps records—the danger signals warning him that all is not well. He will, by acting promptly, hold his losses to a minimum, and await more favorable market conditions, or trade on the short side of the market.

When a stock starts sliding downward, no one can tell how far it will go. Nor can anyone guess the ultimate top on a stock in a broad upward movement. Livermore recommended a few thoughts that should be kept uppermost in the trader's mind.

Never sell a stock because it seems high-priced. You may watch the stock go from 10 to 50 and decide that it is selling at too high a level. This is the time to determine whether anything will prevent it from starting at 50 and going to 150 under favorable earning conditions and good corporate management. Many have lost their capital funds by selling a stock short after a seemingly too high, long upward movement. Study the stock on the basis of current conditions, looking for a clear reason to sell.

By contrast, never buy a stock simply because it has had a big decline in price. The decline is probably based on a very good reason. For example, the stock may still be selling at an extremely high price relative to its value—even if the current level seems low.

Livermore's trading method may come as a surprise to most traders. When he saw, by studying his records, that an upward trend was in progress, he became a buyer as soon as the stock made a new high on its movement, after having had a normal reaction.

The same applies whenever he took the short side. Why? Because he was following the current trend direction, and his records signaled him to go ahead. It was a safe trade.

The Livermore trading system insists that *it is foolhardy to make a second trade, if your first trade shows you a loss.*

As an ironclad Livermore rule, *never average losses.* Let that thought be written indelibly and forever upon your mind.

Some 2004 examples of blue chip stocks reinforce Livermore's own words. (See Figures 2.4–2.10.) There are no good stocks—only stocks that make you money. Some people considered these stocks as unassailable . . . safe as money in the bank. These blue chip stocks include:

- General Electric
- Coke
- Lucent
- General Motors
- Microsoft
- Sun Microsystems
- Intel

Perhaps these blue chip gilt edged stocks will come back in the future, but there is no doubt they will need many years to recover. The emotional hell of their owners is inestimable.

Figure 2.4 A current (2004) example of a stock considered a good (blue chip) stock.

21

22

Figure 2.5 A current (2004) example of a stock considered a good (blue chip) stock.

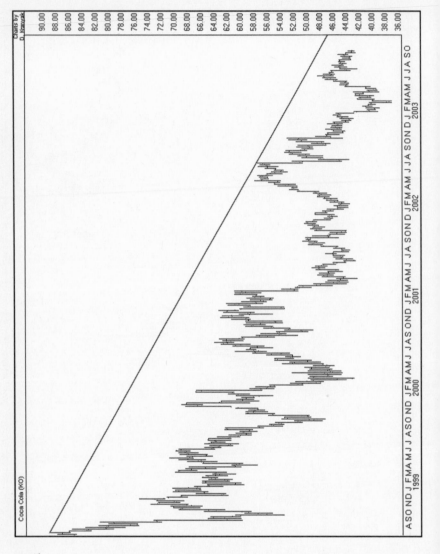

Coca Cola (KO)

Charts by
D. Izraylevski

ASO ND JFMAMJ JASOND JFMAMJ JASOND JFMAMJ JASOND JFMAMJ JASOND JFMAMJ JASO
1999   2000   2001   2002   2003

90.00
88.00
86.00
84.00
82.00
80.00
78.00
76.00
74.00
72.00
70.00
68.00
66.00
64.00
62.00
60.00
58.00
56.00
54.00
52.00
50.00
48.00
46.00
44.00
42.00
40.00
38.00
36.00

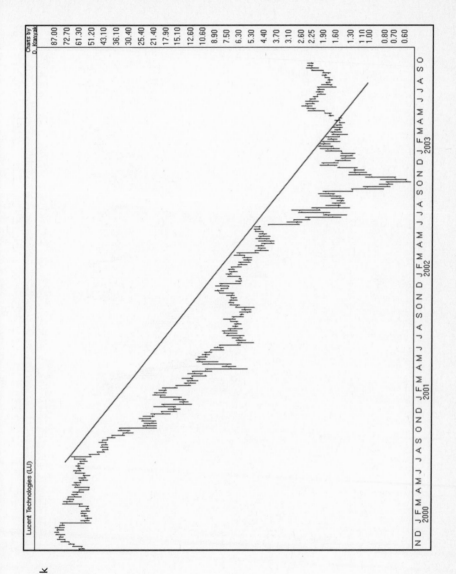

Figure 2.6 A current (2004) example of a stock considered a good (blue chip) stock.

24

Figure 2.7 A current (2004) example of a stock considered a good (blue chip) stock.

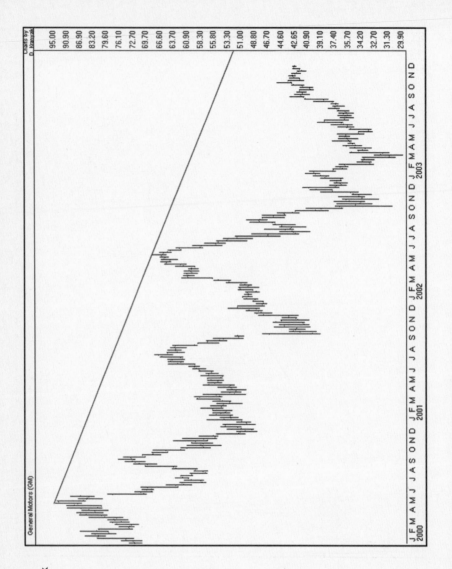

General Motors (GM)

J F M A M J J A S O N D J F M A M J J A S O N D J F M A M J J A S O N D J F M A M J J A S O N D
2000　　　　　　　　　2001　　　　　　　　2002　　　　　　　　2003

95.00
90.90
86.90
83.20
79.60
76.10
72.70
69.70
66.60
63.70
60.90
58.30
55.80
53.30
51.00
48.80
46.70
44.60
42.65
40.90
39.10
37.40
35.70
34.20
32.70
31.30
29.90

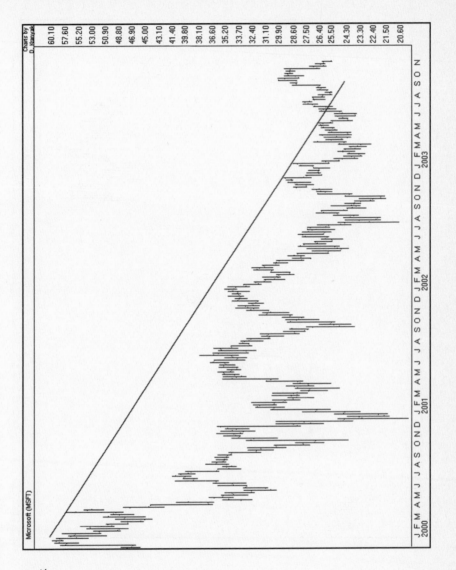

Figure 2.8 A current (2004) example of a stock considered a good (blue chip) stock.

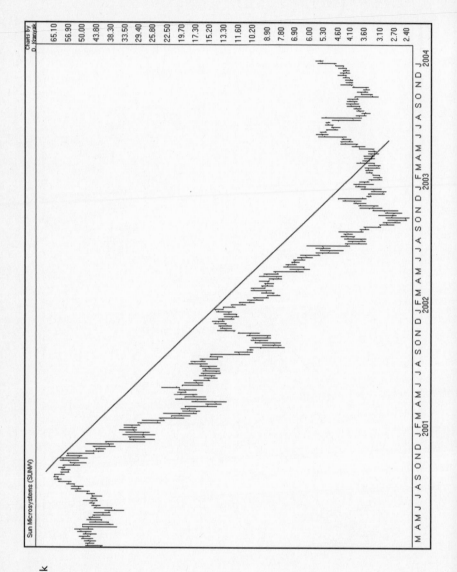

Figure 2.9 A current (2004)example of a stock considered a good (blue chip) stock.

Figure 2.10 A current (2004) example of a stock considered a good (blue chip) stock.

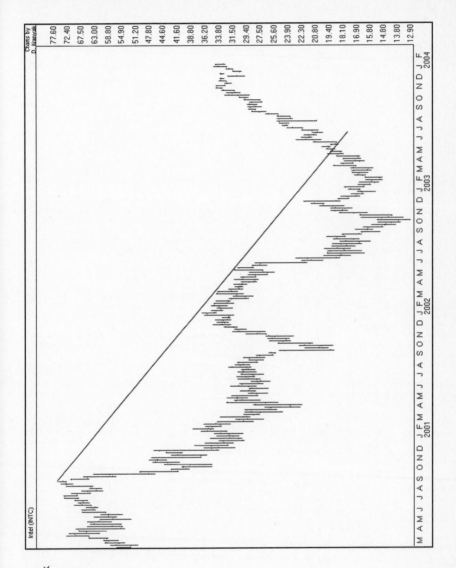

CHAPTER 3

Livermore Trading Discoveries

The stock market is forever evolving—it is dynamic. Because of its complexity, Livermore believed that a stock trader is "Always a student, never a master." As Livermore gained knowledge over his 45 years of trading, he modified his trading system accordingly. He always reviewed and studied each of his trades, good or bad. He went to school on his successes and his failures. They always had a lesson for him, sometimes hidden, sometimes painful.

DISCOVERY 1: TRADE ONLY THE LEADERS

Once he was sure he was correct in his conclusions, he would incorporate them into his trading system. One early Livermore lesson was "trade only the leaders in any particular industry group." Don't play in the junkyard with the weaker stocks. Don't try to fish for the bargain stock, the as yet undiscovered stock in an industry group. Rather, go with the proven leaders! In the long run, you will be much better off. This single piece of advice can greatly assist a trader in the decision-making process. If you cannot make money with the leaders of a stock group, it is unlikely that you can make money at all in that group.

He believed there is always the temptation in the stock market, particularly after a period of success, to become careless or excessively ambitious. Prudent trading requires the trader to use sound common sense and clear thinking to keep the profit that he has already made in the market. If you will hold fast to sound principles, you will not lose your money, once you have acquired it.

Everyone knows that stock prices move up and down. They always have, and they always will. Livermore believed that behind these major movements is an irresistible force: a momentum like a wave of water, in some cases a tidal wave that once set in motion would remain in motion until it hit an obstacle and stopped or was reversed—in stock trading this is know as "the trend."

Noticing and observing this power is all one needs to do. It is not profitable to be too curious about all the reasons behind the force of price movements. You risk the danger of clouding your mind with nonessentials. Just recognize that the movement, the power, the momentum is there, and take advantage of it by steering your speculative ship along with the tide. Use the power. Do not argue with the market you are observing, and most of all, do not try to combat it.

Remember also that it is dangerous to start spreading out all over the market, carrying several positions. Do not have an interest in too many stocks at any one time. It is much easier to watch a few than many. Livermore made this mistake of owning too many stocks early in his career, and it cost him money. He believed the most stocks that can be handled at any one time was 10, but he felt much safer and in control if the number was smaller, say no more than 5 stocks.

Another mistake he recognized and warned against was to turn completely bearish or bullish on the whole market. Because one stock in some particular group had clearly reversed its course from the general market trend, don't assume from this that the entire market is changing in trend.

Rather, be patient, and wait until you see other groups turning to a new direction, particularly the leading industry groups within the market. The time to act is when these other groups corroborate the actions of the first group and indicate a decline or advance in the direction of the market, showing that a new trend is forming. If you use the Livermore trading system principles, you will have plenty of time to see the trend changing. In time, other stocks will clearly give you the same indication. Those are the cues you must wait for, and you must take them when they show themselves. These were the specific cues Livermore got in the Crash of 1907, when he made $3 million in a single day, and in the Crash of 1929, when he profited by more than $100 million by being on the short side.

Back in the wild bull markets of the late 1920s (before the Crash of 1929), he saw clearly that the advance in the copper stocks had come to an end. Copper was a major commodity used as a bellwether in the 1920s to predict the market, because it was so widely used in the building industry. Many of today's traders still use copper in their calculations to predict market direction.

In 1929, Livermore next noticed that the advance in the motor group had reached its zenith, stopped dead in its tracks, and rolled over. Because the bull market in those two industry groups had ended, he arrived at the faulty conclusion that he could safely sell everything and jump on the short side. He was wrong. The rest of the market kept moving in its upward spiral. Livermore lost his shirt on these trades.

But at the same time he was piling up huge profits on his copper and motor short sales. Overall, he was about breaking even. He persisted in his short positions on the entire market and continued to lose on these trades. He spent the next six months of 1929 trying to find the top of the utility group, another key bellwether group. Eventually, this and other industry groups reached their peaks. By that time, Anaconda copper was selling 50 points below its previous high and the motor stocks were in close to the same ratio. So the profits on these short sales continued to climb, offsetting his losses, but not by much.

The lesson to impress upon your mind is that when you clearly see a move coming in a particular industry group, act upon it. But do not let yourself automatically act in the same way in another industry group until you plainly see signs that the second group is in a position to follow the trend of the first group you are trading. The trader must have patience and wait until his judgment is confirmed by the market. In time, you will get the same tip-off in other groups that you received in the first group. Just don't spread out your positions and move to trade the entire market, until you have first received confirmation.

Confine your studies of movements only to the prominent stocks of the day, the leaders. If you cannot make money out of the leading active issues in the leading industry groups, you are not going to make money out of the stock market as a whole. If a trader had followed Livermore's advice in the last crash (1999), he would have seen history repeat itself as the leading stocks and groups such as Amazon, Yahoo, America Online, Lucent, Cisco Systems, Sun Microsystems, and even the great Microsoft reached their highs and rolled over, leading the entire market with them. The signals from these stocks came three to six months before the entire market followed suit. Livermore knew well that the market leaders in a strong bull market are the first to go up and the first to roll over and go down. Rarely are the market leaders of one bull market the same as the leaders of the new bull market, when it finally rallies and begins its new cycle. The same will be true in this market of the new millennium.

Livermore always identified the market leaders and tracked them very closely. He also spent a lot of time deducing who would be the new leaders in a new market. If he were alive today, he would have already figured out what stocks will be the leaders of this new millennium market. A prudent trader of today would be wise to do the same. Find the new markets, the new products, and the new market leaders before the crowd.

Just as styles in women's clothing are forever changing, the old stock market leaders drop out, and new ones rise up to take their places. In the 1920s, the chief leaders were the railroads, American sugar, and tobacco. Then along came the steels, and sugar and tobacco were nudged into the background. Every new market cycle has new market leaders, with few if any of the old leaders remaining in the picture. Livermore believed it would always be that way as long as there was a stock market.

Note this Livermore trading rule: New leaders emerge with each new market. At this current moment, new leaders are moving into positions of leadership.

Also note another Livermore rule: It is not prudent for a trader to try and keep account of too many stocks at one time. You will become entangled and confused. Try to analyze comparatively few groups and few stocks. You will find it is much easier to obtain a true picture that way than if you tried to dissect the entire market.

If you analyze correctly the course of two stocks in the four or five prominent groups, you need not worry about what the rest are going to do. It becomes the old story of follow the leader . . . keep mentally flexible. Remember the leaders of today may not be the leaders two years from now.

The skilled trader will study only a limited number of groups and the leading stocks in each of those groups. He will learn to look carefully before he leaps. In other words, he will be patient. After 1920, a new age of markets was ushered in—one that offered safer opportunities for the reasonable, studious, competent investor and speculator. There were technology improvements for that age with the invention of the widely used ticker tape, the telephone, and newspapers that provided a current record of the stock trades and activity posted every day along with headlines and editorials. This all helped traders and investors make intelligent decisions on what to buy.

DISCOVERY 2: UNDERSTAND INDUSTRY GROUP MOVEMENTS

Livermore found that industry group movement was the key to individual stock movement. In the 1920s, he made a very important discovery that he applied to his trading system: Stocks did not move alone. When they moved, they moved in sectors and industry groups. For Livermore, this was a huge breakthrough.

If U.S. Steel rose, then sooner or later Bethlehem, Republic, and Crucible would follow. Livermore observed this time and time again, and it became one of the most important trading weapons in his arsenal. As a result, Livermore never tracked a single stock. He first tracked the industry group movements. Livermore decided that a legitimate group movement had to include at least the two leaders of the group, and eventually all the stocks in the group would follow.

It is a commonplace mistake for traders of today to confuse Industry Groups and Industry Sectors. In fact the media and traders often use these terms interchangeably. It is very important to know the difference.

Sector means all the industry groups within a particular section or area. As examples, the Financial Sector includes a number of Groups, as do the Computer, Communications, and Medical Sectors.

In the Financial Sector, for example, there are national banks, regional banks, savings and loan banks, financial service groups, stock brokers, and others. The Computer Sector includes, among others, box makers, software providers, makers of peripherals such as printers, monitors, and hand-held devices.

Livermore believed that the most intelligent way to get one's mind attuned to market conditions and to be successful in trading was to make a deep and through study of industry groups in order to differentiate the good groups from the bad. The action result was this: Buy groups in a promising position and short Industry Groups that are not.

It has been shown time and time again that on Wall Street *people very often fail to see the thing that is right in front of them.*

—Jesse Livermore

Currently there are more than 87 million Americans invested in the stock market in one form or another. It cannot be emphasized too strongly the importance of first understanding the Industry Group action before the purchase of any single security. It was a key to Livermore's incredible success in trading the market. This key factor is understood by some of today's market participants, but seemingly ignored by a large number traders and investors.

Stay away from weak groups! Conversely, just as Livermore would have avoided the weak stocks in the weak industry groups, he favored the strongest stocks in the strongest industries. The trader must, of course, be able and willing to revise any forecasts and positions in the light of

developments that occur from day to day and to move quickly, if factors
have moved against him. This is just good common sense.

Why Industry Groups Move Together

If you were to ask today's market pundits why industry groups move together, you would be subjected to a lengthy, probably convoluted, answer.
Like many other aspects of his market views, the group movement
premise was quite simple to Livermore. He explained it in one sentence:
"If the basic reasons are sound why U.S. Steel's business should come into
favor in the stock market, then the rest of the steel group should also follow for the same basic reasons." The converse to this premise, of course,
also works for playing the short side of the market: When a group goes out
of favor for a common basic set of reasons, just as it went into favor, it
will include all the stocks in that industry group.

The industry group charts in Figures 3.1–3.3 illustrate the general di-

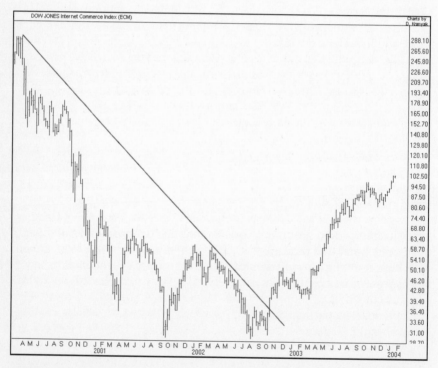

Figure 3.1 This is the first in the series of industry group charts, all showing
the general direction of the group. This is the Internet Group.

Figure 3.2 This is the second in the series of industry group charts, all showing the general direction of the group. This is the Broker/Dealers Group.

rection of three current groups: The Internet Group, the Broker/Dealers, and the Housing Group.

Note: It was also an important clue for Livermore that, if a particular stock in the favored group did not move up and prosper with the others, this could mean that perhaps this particular stock was weak or sick, and therefore might be a good short sale or at the very least, the trader should be cautious in buying it. It can act as a red warning flag that the stock may be in trouble.

The only exception to group movement is when a single stock may comprise over 50 percent or more of the total sales of the group, as is currently the case with Intel and Microsoft, who dominate their Industry Groups. In these examples, you do not need to examine the two leading stocks in the industry group; one will do the job, because sooner or later the rest of the group must follow the single dominant leader.

Figure 3.3 This is the third in the series of industry group charts, all showing the general direction of the group. This is the Housing Group.

Also note this may not always be the expected, conventional stock in the group. Occasionally, a smaller, well-managed stock will assume leadership, perhaps with a new product or strategy, and may knock out the old leader. Keep alert! Choose the most powerful stock in the group, not the best bargain or a beaten down stock poised to recover.

DISCOVERY 3: TOP DOWN TRADING

The concept of Top Down Trading is very straight forward, involving four steps.

Step 1—Set Up the Checklist

Before making any trade on any particular stock, you must first check off the following items:

First, check the line of least resistance to establish the overall current market direction. Remember, Livermore never used the terms bull or bear because they forced a mind-set that he believed made his thinking less flexible. He used the term *line of least resistance.* He checked to see if the current line of least resistance was positive, negative or neutral—sideways. Be sure to check the exact market the stock trades on—for instance, does the stock you are interested in trade on the Dow, the Nasdaq, or the Amex? Establish this before executing the trade.

It is essential to make sure the lines of least resistance are in the direction of your trade before entering the trade. See Figure 3.4 where the Nasdaq formed a pivot point and changed basic direction.

Figure 3.4 Here the Nasdaq formed a pivot point and changed basic direction.

Step 2: Track the Industry Group

Check the specific Industry Group. If you are considering a trade in AT&T, check out the Telecommunications Long Distance Group. If Haliburton is your trade of choice, check out the Oil Well Drilling Group. If you are looking at a trade in Harrah's Entertainment, check out the Leisure Gambling Group. Make sure the group is moving in the correct direction, the line of least resistance, in order to increase your chance of a profit on the trade you have selected. In the example below, the trade is in the Internet Industry Group.

The Internet Industry Group began its recovery in February/March of 2003, the same time as the Nasdaq. (See Figure 3.5.) In March/April, it gave a clear sign that the line of least resistance was upward. The signals confirmed each other that the trend was now to the upside.

Figure 3.5 The Internet Industry Group began its recovery in February/March of 2003, the same time as the Nasdaq.

Step 3: Tandem Trading

Tandem Trading involves comparing two stocks of the same group. Compare the stock you're interested in trading with the sister stock. For example, if you plan to trade in General Motors, check a sister stock such as Ford or Chrysler/Mercedes. If you are going to trade Best Buy, than check Circuit City—a sister stock.

Tandem Trading Example: The stocks chosen for this example are Morgan Stanley and Merrill Lynch—the two leaders in the Broker/Dealer Group. Both stocks bottomed out in February/March of 2003 and gave a signal, by pivotal point, that the line of least resistance was positive. Because the broker/dealers are also often an important bellwether group for what the market may do in the future, this chart action (see Figure 3.6) was a precursor of what was to come in the overall markets.

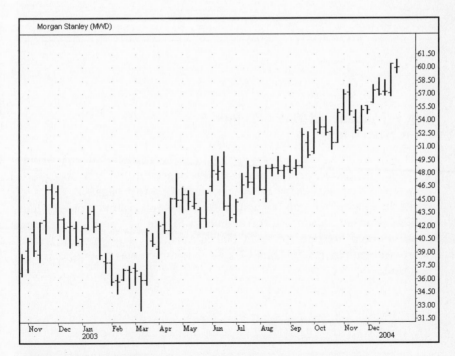

Figure 3.6 Both Morgan Stanley and Merrill Lynch bottomed out in February/March of 2003 and gave a pivotal point signal that the line of least resistance was positive.

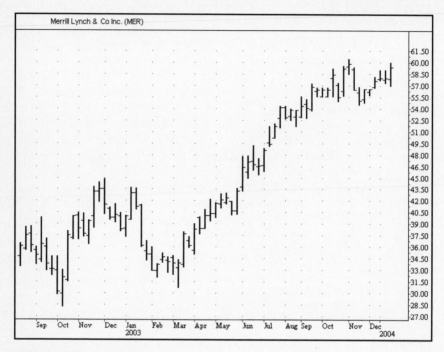

Figure 3.6   *(Continued)*

Step 4: Examine All Three Factors at the Same Time

Look at the market, the Industry Group, and the Tandem Industry Group stocks in one glance. (The example of this is seen in the new Livermore Software from Stock Market Solutions, on the opposite page.)

In the example, it can be clearly seen how the system works, when all factors are in unison. All the signals in Figure 3.7 (both market and stock) show a bottoming out in March/April and a reversal in trend, clearly indicating that the line of least resistance was now upward in direction.

NOTES FOR THE TRADER

Due Diligence: Do a final, thorough analysis of the individual stock you have decided to trade. This step would be similar to traveling down

Figure 3.7 All the signals (both market and stocks) show a bottoming out in March/April and a reversal in trend, clearly indicating that the line of least resistance was now upward in direction. The group is the broker/dealers with Morgan Stanley and Merrill Lynch as the two leading stocks in that group.

the runway—but not lift off—a final chance to change your mind before you pull the trigger and buy the stock. This final step must be completed by you, and you alone. Make this decision on your own—it's your money.

A military friend of mine, U.S. Navy Commander (Ret.) Dennis Kranyak, compares this approach of Livermore's to the steps the U.S. Marines follow before they select a beach to assault. They study all the factors on all the possible beaches. They analyze all these factors as carefully as they can with the full knowledge that the assault will not be perfect, no matter what the analysis reveals to them.

There will always be unknown factors, the main one being the unpredictable human factor in assaulting a beach or playing the stock market . . . there is always the *human factor* to consider.

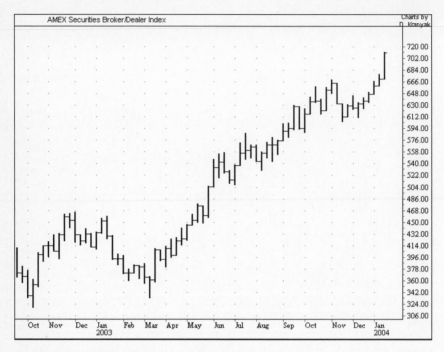

Figure 3.7 *(Continued)*

Here are some Livermore Laws:

- Wait until the preponderance of evidence is in your favor.
- Use Top Down Trading.
- Be patient! —Jesse Livermore

SUMMARY

Tandem Trading, the use of sister stocks, was one of the great secrets of Livermore's trading techniques and remains just as valid today as it did in years gone by. This technique is an essential element in both Top Down Trading and in the maintenance of the trade after it has been completed. Livermore never looked at a single stock in a vacuum—rather, he looked at the top two stocks in an Industry Group and did his analysis on both

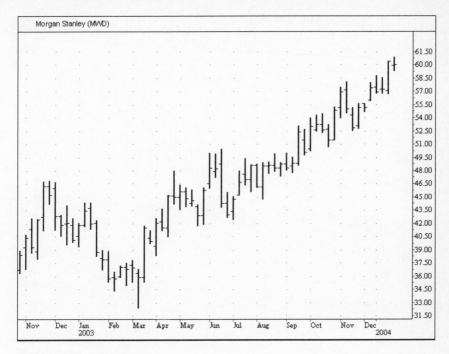

Figure 3.7 *(Continued)*

stocks. Understanding Top Down Trading, including Tandem Trading or sister stock trading, is essential to the successful use of the Livermore Trading System. The overall conclusion was simple: both stocks had to have the same pattern to initiate a trade in that group.

Never look at only one stock—look at two—track two. Why? Because stocks in the same group should always move together. Tracking two stocks instead of one adds a great confirming psychological dimension to your trading. You will discover when you visualize two stocks moving in unison that they confirm the movements of each other. It is twice as hard *not* to follow the correct signal when you see with your own eyes that the sister stocks actually move in tandem and therefore give you the absolute confirmation.

It was this Tandem Trading technique that allowed Livermore to police his investments properly. Once the investment was made, Livermore heightened his vigilance and continued his due diligence by daily observation of the two stocks.

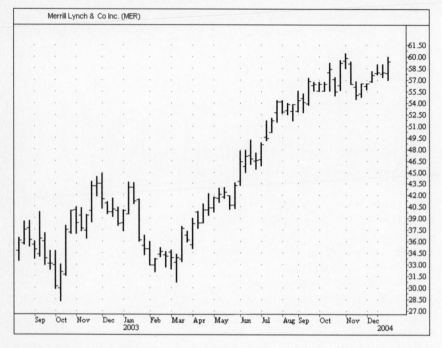

Figure 3.7   *(Continued)*

For Livermore, the evidence, the clues, the truth were always in the market itself—quite visible if a person knew how to read them, the way an experienced forensic investigator examines the details of a crime scene—clues become obvious to him that are visible to no one else. The answer lies in the market facts—the challenge for the trader is to properly interpret the facts that appear. He told his sons: "It's like being a great detective working on a great case that never ends—you never know it all!"

Several other Livermore principles are at work in his Top Dawn Trading method and were part of his checklist:

 ► *Always trade with the trend.* A trader should always have the trending wind at his back. Find the market that the stock is traded in (Dow, S&P, Amex, Nasdaq) and observe how the overall market is trading. For example, examine the line of least resistance or the trend of the Nasdaq, if you are interested in trading Microsoft (MSFT) or Intel (INTC). Or examine the Standard and Poor's 500 (SPY'S) if you are interested in trading the top 500 stocks in America. The ultimate objective in the trade is to have the overall market trending in the same direction as your trade. You can trade short or long as long as it coincides with the current trend at the time. Livermore never cared which side of the market he was on—short or long—it was all the same to him.

▶ *Only play the leading stocks in the leading Industry Groups.* In other words, only *follow the leaders.*

CALLING THE TOPS OF MARKETS USING INDUSTRY GROUPS AND TOP DOWN TRADING

Livermore was asked many times how he called the top of the overall market, as he did in 1907 and 1929 when he made millions by going short. He did it using his Top Down Trading System along with his Industry Group Analysis method. This gave him the clues that enabled him to call these major changes in market direction.

It was Livermore's experience that stock-group behavior is an important key to overall market direction, a key known by Wall Street, but ignored by most traders, whether they are big or small. He believed the groups often provided the key to changes in trends. As the favored groups of the moment became weaker and collapsed, a correction in the overall market was usually on the way. *Note:* The same thing happened in the 2000 market collapse. The leaders flipped and fell first, and the others followed.

CHAPTER 4

Livermore Pattern Recognition Timing Keys

Pivotal Point Trading

Pivotal Points are the perfect psychological moment to make a trade. Reversal Pivotal Points mark a change in trend.

—Jesse Livermore

REVERSAL PIVOTAL POINTS

Reversal Pivotal Points are a key factor in the Livermore Trading System. Livermore was the first person to use the term Pivotal Point and incorporate it as an important part of his trading system.

He never wanted to buy at the lowest price or sell at the top. He wanted to buy at the right time and sell at the right time. The Pivotal Point Trading theory allowed Livermore the chance to buy at the right time. But this also required him to have patience and wait for the perfect trading situation to develop. If all the right conditions did not coincide on a particular stock he was following, he didn't care, because the proper pattern would sooner or later appear on another stock. Patience . . . patience . . . patience—wait for the perfect trade—that was his key to timing success.

Livermore always considered *time* as a real and essential trading element. He often said: "It's not the thinkin' that makes the money—it's the sittin' and the waitin' that makes the money."

This often has been incorrectly interpreted by many people to mean Livermore would buy a stock, and then sit and wait for it to move. This is not so. What he meant was there were many occasions when he sat and waited in cash, until the right situation appeared. When these conditions came together, when as many of the odds as possible were in his favor, then and only then, like a cobra, he would strike, usually with great results.

Buying on the Pivotal Point assured him the best chance of coming into the situation *just as the action was about to begin.* And once he was sure of his play, he wasn't afraid to make his commitment. He wasn't called the Boy Plunger for nothing.

It was Livermore's firm conviction that when a speculator can determine the Pivotal Point of a stock and plan the action at that point, he may make a commitment with the positive assurance of being right from the start.

But bear in mind, when using Pivotal Points to anticipate movements, that if the stock does not perform as it should after crossing the Pivotal Point, this is an important danger signal that must be heeded immediately. Every time Livermore lost patience and failed to await the Pivotal Points, every time he fiddled around for easy profits, he lost money.

The study of Pivotal Points is fascinating, providing a golden array of opportunities for personal research. The trader can derive a singular pleasure and satisfaction from successful trades based on his own judgment. You will discover that profits made in this way are immensely more gratifying than any that could possibly come from tips, or the guidance of someone else. If you make your own discovery, trade your own way, exercise patience, and watch for the danger signals, you will ultimately begin thinking like a successful trader. The Pivotal Points theory applies to commodity trading as well as stock trading. Livermore never considered this theory as a foolproof, perfect method of picking winners, but it does represent an *essential part* of the Livermore trading system. Pivotal Points are vital as the confirming signal that your judgment is correct, but you must let them play out.

No trader is right all the time on the market. On occasion, the market will move contrary to what a speculator has predicted. At these times, the successful speculator must abandon his predictions, and follow the market action. A prudent speculator never argues with the tape. Remember what Livermore preached: *Markets are never wrong—opinions often are.*

The Crash of 1929 brought about Livermore's complete belief in Pivotal Points. Black Tuesday was the biggest Pivotal Point in the history of the stock market—the market fell 11.7 percent in one single day. This would represent a drop of 1100 points on the Dow in a single day in today's market.

Livermore said that once he understood Pivotal Points they became one of the true trading keys, a reliable trading technique that was basically unknown, in a formal way, to stock speculators of the twenties and early thirties and is to this day hardly used by traders. Pivotal Points are a *timing* device that can be used to get in and out of the market with great success.

The Reversal Pivotal Point is not easily defined. In Livermore's mind it was "a change in basic market direction—the perfect psychological time in basic market direction—the perfect psychological time at the beginning of a new move, representing a major change in the basic trend."

For Livermore's style of trading it did not matter if a stock was at the bottom or the top of a long-term trending move, because he would buy or sell any stock, going long or short at any time.

The *Reversal Pivotal Point* flagged the optimal trading timing for him. Figures 4.1 and 4.2 show the Reversal Pivotal Point.

Figure 4.1 This is the first of two examples that show the *Reversal Pivotal Point*. For Yahoo! the Reversal Pivotal Point came in October.

Figure 4.2   This is the second of two examples that show the *Reversal Pivotal Point*. For Merrill Lynch the Reversal Pivotal Point came in March.

Volume Factors

Reversal Pivotal Points are almost always accompanied by a heavy increase in volume, a climax of buying, which is met with a barrage of selling—or vice-versa. Increased volume is an essential element in understanding Pivotal Points—it is usually present and confirms the Pivotal Point. This battle between buyers and sellers causes the stock to reverse its direction, top out, or bottom out in a decline. In effect, it has changed momentum and is at the start of a new trend direction for the stock. Look for the tell-tale increase in volume. These important confirming volume spurts often end the day with a 50 percent to 500 percent increase in the average daily volume.

Reversal Pivotal Points usually came after long-term trending moves. This is one of the reasons why Livermore always felt patience was so necessary for success in catching the big moves. You need patience to be sure that you have identified a true Reversal Pivotal Point. He developed the following tests:

> First, he would send out a *probe*. He would buy a small percentage of the overall stock position that he wanted to eventually establish; if he was correct on the first trade, he made a second trade. This strategy is fully explained in the Money Management section of this book.

> He used a second test to confirm whether a Reversal Pivotal Point had truly occurred. He employed his Top Down Trading Procedure and looked at the Industry Group, always looking at the two leading stocks in the group, to see if they had the same pattern as the stock he was interested in trading. This was the final confirmation he needed to confirm that he was on the right track. (See Figure 4.3.)

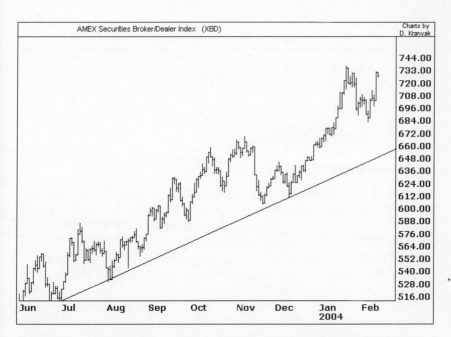

Figure 4.3 When Livermore employed his Top Down Trading Procedure, he looked at the industry group, and then he looked at the two leading stocks in the group, to see if they had the same pattern as the stock he was interested in trading.

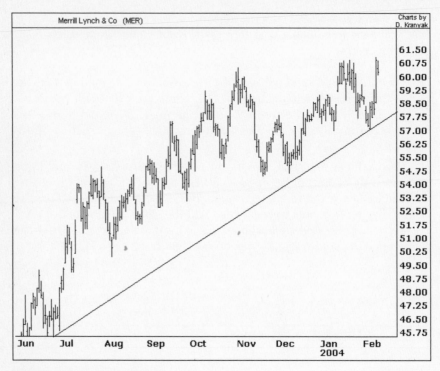

Figure 4.3 *(Continued)*

PIVOTAL POINT TRADING

Evaluating Continuation Pivotal Points

Livermore's Pivotal Point methodology divided Pivotal Points into two categories. The first, which we have already discussed, he called a Reversal Pivotal Point; the second he named the Continuation Pivotal Point.

It is essential to understand that while the Reversal Pivotal Point marks a definite change in direction, the Continuation Pivotal Point confirms that the move is proceeding in the proper direction. Continuation Pivotal Points usually occur during a trending move as a natural reaction for a stock in a definite trend. A pattern is forming that demonstrates support or resistance lines. The trader must wait as this formation builds to determine if the pattern will develop into a support area. Or if the stock breaks out on the downside, this may be the area of resistance line in the next move upward.

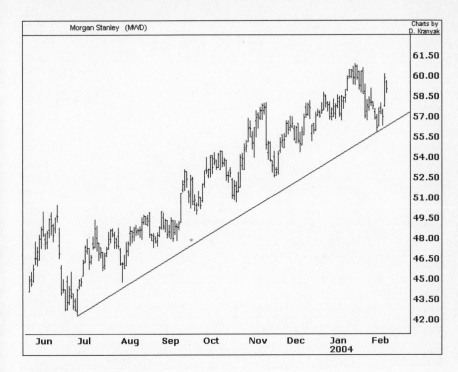

Figure 4.3 *(Continued)*

As has been stated so many times before in this book, never anticipate the market move, simply wait for the move to be revealed to you by the action of the stock. The Continuation Pivotal Point is a potential additional entry point in an ongoing move—it provides a signal, a chance, to increase your position. Of course, the stock must emerge from the Continuation Pivotal Point headed in the same direction it was in before the correction. If not, this is a clear signal to close out your position.

Most importantly, Livermore defined a Continuation Pivotal Point as a consolidation in which the stock pauses and takes a breather in its ascent. It gives a stock a chance to consolidate, often allowing a stock's ratio of earnings and sales to catch up to its current price. It is usually a natural reaction in the stock's progress. The prudent trader, however, will carefully observe which way the stock will emerge from this consolidation, and not anticipate. (See Figure 4.4.)

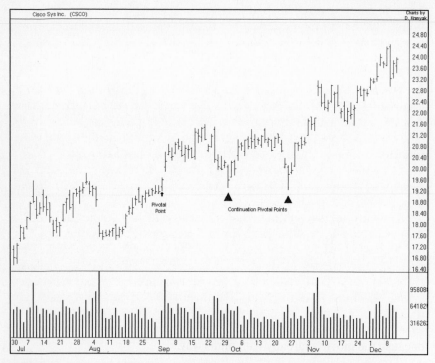

Figure 4.4   The Continuation Pivotal Point is usually a natural reaction or
pause in the stock's progress. The prudent trader, however, will carefully
observe which way the stock will emerge from this consolidation, and
not anticipate.

For Livermore, a stock's price is never too high to buy or too low
to sell short. Waiting for these Continuation Pivotal Points signals
gave him the opportunity to either open a new position or to add to
a current position. Do not chase a stock if it gets away from you—let
it go.

Livermore would rather wait and pay more, after the stock had re-
grouped and formed a new Continuation Pivotal Point, because this provides a confirmation and mental insurance that the stock will most likely
continue with its move.

Conversely, this Pivotal Point theory can also uncover successful
short-selling opportunities. Livermore looked for stocks that traded

down to a new low for the last year or so. If they formed a False Pivotal Point, that is, if they rallied from this new low and then dropped down through and formed another new low, they were most likely to continue down from there and establish additional new lows for the move.

By correctly catching either the Reversal Pivotal Points or the Continuation Pivotal Point, Livermore was able to make his initial purchase so that he had an entry point at the right price from the beginning of the move. This ensured that he was never in a loss position and could therefore ride out the normal stock fluctuations without risking his own capital. Once the stock had moved off the Pivotal Point Livermore was only risking his paper profits, not his actual capital, because he was "in profit" from the beginning of the trade.

His early years of getting crushed because he had bought the stock at the wrong time in its move helped him formulate his unique theory of Pivotal Points. On many of those early trades he was "never in profit." If a trader buys before the Pivotal Point is established, he may be early. This is dangerous because the stock may never form a proper Pivotal Point to establish its direction clearly. But the trader must be careful—please note that if you buy more than 5 percent to 10 percent above the initial Reversal Pivotal Point, you may be too late. You may have lost your trading edge because the move is already well underway.

The Pivotal Point (either the Reversal or the Continuation point) is the only tip-off you need to trade and win. A trader has to be patient, because it takes time for a stock to run its logical and natural course and form a proper Pivotal Point. (See Figures 4.5 and 4.6.) It will not be willed or forced forward by an impatient trader. It will come as a natural event. Be Patient!

Trade only on the Pivotal Points. I always made money when I was patient and traded on the Pivotal Points.

—Jesse Livermore

Livermore also firmly believed that often the largest part of a stock movement occurred in the last two weeks or so of the trade—he named it the Final Mark-up Phase. The same thing applies for commodities. So, once again, a trader must be patient, get into position and wait, but at the same time he must be completely alert for the clues when they come, good or bad, and then take action to either buy or sell his position.

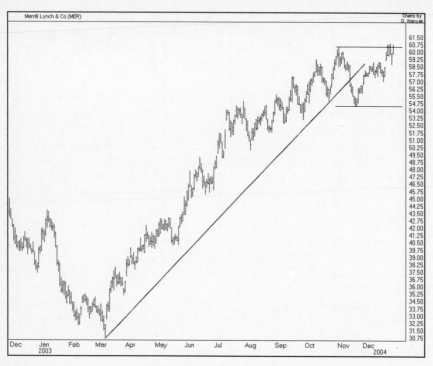

Figure 4.5 The Pivotal Point (either the reversal or the continuation point) gives the only tip-off you need to trade and win.

UNDERSTANDING TREND LINES AND PIVOTAL POINTS

Trend lines are one of the oldest tools used by technical traders. They are easily charted, readable, reliable and very useful. They easily can be employed in conjunction with the Livermore Theory. The key is to recognize whether a line shows a true change in the basic trend of a stock or simply a normal reaction. (See Figures 4.7 and 4.8.)

The trend lines are formed between the relative highs and the relative lows of a stock's trading pattern. They form a channel within which the stock trades. This channel supplies the trader with a picture of the sup-

Figure 4.6 Another chart showing the Pivotal Point. A trader has to be patient, because it takes time for a stock to run out its logical and natural course and form a proper Pivotal Point. It will not be willed or forced forward by an impatient trader. It will come as a natural event.

port and resistance channel. Support is usually identified by a previous re-action low causing the stock to be supported at this old low. Resistance is the opposite of support. It represents a price level or an area above the market where selling pressure simply overpowers buying power and the stock is turned back or repelled at this level, retreating usually back into the trough.

Usually, when the trend lines are broken, the stock will continue to trade in the direction of the breakout. It should be noted that this can be in either direction. These trend lines can be formed and identified in all time frames.

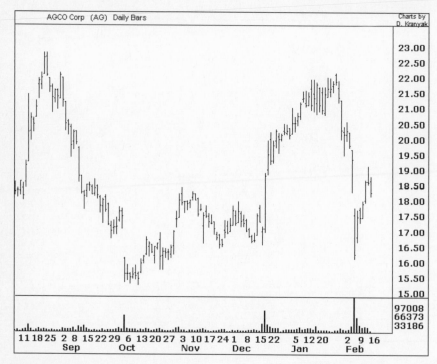

Figure 4.7 The trend lines are formed between the relative highs and the relative lows of a stock's trading pattern. Break-outs occur when the trend line is broken.

In Figures 4.9 and 4.10, we are using 10 days, and a 6-month time frame for the same stock. All these various time frames can be success-fully traded. The volatility of the stock is in direct proportion to the tim-ing—the shorter the time frame, say one day, the more volatile the stock movements.

Because trend lines have been around forever and are very simple to use, many traders do not spend a lot of time and energy on them. This was a mistake as far as Livermore was concerned because the trend lines can give the trader a clear picture of the momentum be-hind a stock—up, down, or sideways, and they clearly define the chan-nel within which a stock moves—this makes it far easier for the trader to see when the stock breaks out and when it breaks down—out of the channel.

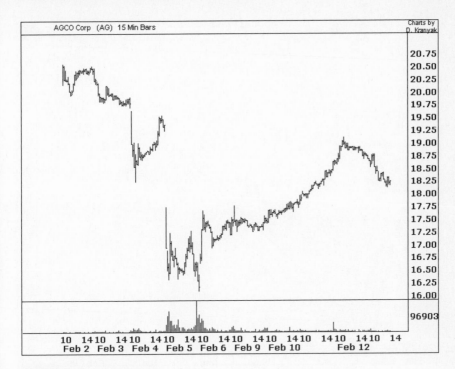

Figure 4.7 *(Continued)*

It should be noted that Livermore did not use charts. He used his complex mathematical formulas (explained in the Secret Market Key section of this book (Chapter 11)) to achieve the same effect. Charts now are used to illustrate the Livermore Trading System details because they are easily available to the trader and have become far more accessible and improved today.

As stated, the Reversal Pivotal Points are really the beginning and end points of trend lines. They appear when the trend is reversing. Figure 4.11 of the Nasdaq clearly shows a Reversal Pivotal Point at the arrow in November/December. Figure 4.12 of Best Buy shows a clear Pivotal Point in November/December.

Continuation Pivotal Points, on the other hand, indicate that a new formation is appearing, although the direction has not yet been

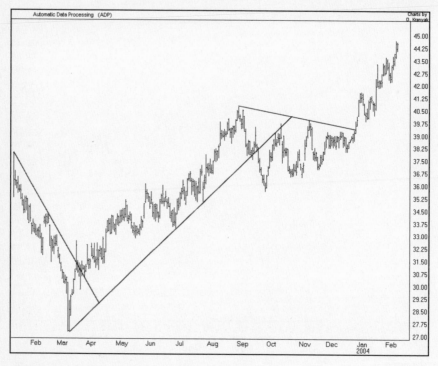

Figure 4.8 This chart is another clear example of trend lines and break-outs.

established. When these form, the trader has a terrific opportunity to wait and see what is next in store for the stocks. The Continuation Pivotal Point for Merrill Lynch appears in August/September and goes on to climb higher in Figure 4.13. Figure 4.14 shows Verisign with two Continuation Pivotal Points in November/February and June/December.

With a little practice, the ordinary trader will soon become skilled at drawing in these trend lines. The results, with patience, can be outstanding. When the Continuation Pivotal Points form, the trader must battle with himself not to anticipate the break-out by superimposing his own logic onto the situation. He must sit on his hands and wait for the confir-

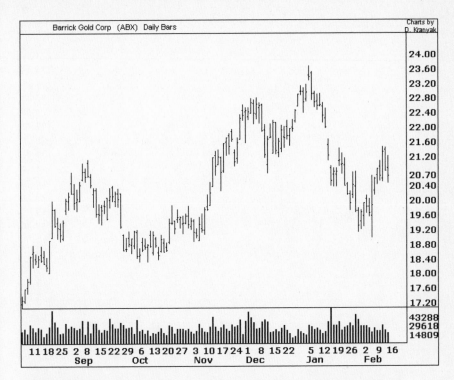

Figure 4.9 In this first of two examples, we are using 10 days, and a 6-month time frame for the same stock. All these various time frames can be successfully traded. The volatility of the stock is in direct proportion to the timing—the shorter the time frame, say one day the more volatile the movements of the stock.

mation that the break-out is valid and the direction obvious, even if he misses a few points on the trade.

Figures 4.15 and 4.16 show how trend lines appear and can be drawn in a trending stock. The Livermore trader wants to seek out trending stocks with low volatility. The first chart, Merrill Lynch, is a trending stock and can be fairly easily read and traded on its pivotal points. The second chart, Microsoft, is a much more choppy and confused stock with no trend or clear direction.

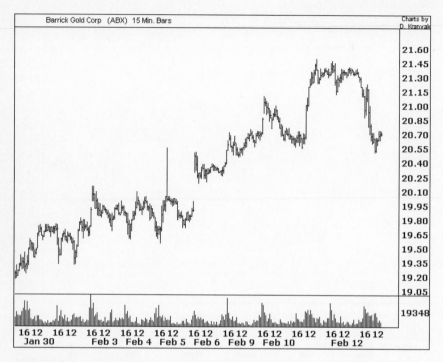

Figure 4.9 *(Continued)*

OTHER RECURRING PATTERNS

Spikes and One-day Reversals

Livermore was very wary of any aberration in the price or volume of a stock that he was tracking. Sometimes, the price would spike, accompanied by abnormally heavy volume of at least a 50 percent increase over the average daily volume. This often led to what he named One-Day Reversals or trading climaxes. They often were like a red flag warning of a change of trend.

An aberration to him was any strong deviation from what was normal for the stock. He considered a spike in the stock price, high volume, as well as low volume, all aberrations, deviations from the norm. To him, these were possible danger signals, and often signals to exit a trade.

The spiking pattern is often a result of pent-up energy in the stock, as in a pressure cooker. It is the follow-through action of the stock that then

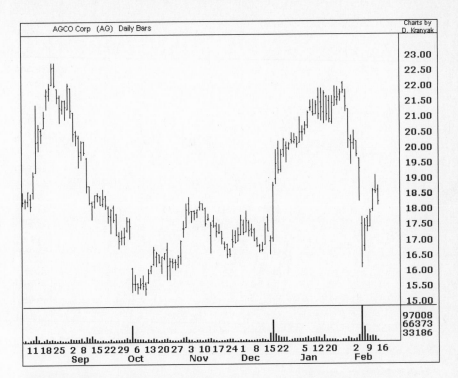

Figure 4.10 In this second of two examples, we are using 10 days, and a 6-month time frame for the same stock. All these various time frames can be successfully traded. The volatility of the stock is in direct proportion to the timing—the shorter the time frame, say one day the more volatile the movements of the stock.

becomes important to observe as to what the next action will be. These spikes are often a reflection of exhaustion in the stock's momentum, and they often appear at the end of a move, like a last gasp. They can provide a terrific signal for the observant, savvy trader.

The *One-Day Reversal* (shown in Figure 4.17) was a strong signal for Livermore, a signal that made him sit up and take notice.

A One-Day Reversal occurs when the high of the day is higher than the high of the previous day, but the close of the day is below the close of the previous day, and the volume of the current day is higher than the volume of the previous day.

This scenario was a potential screaming danger signal to Livermore. Why? Because all during the stock's rise, it followed the trend, the line of least resistance, it had only normal reactions. Then, all of a sudden, it had

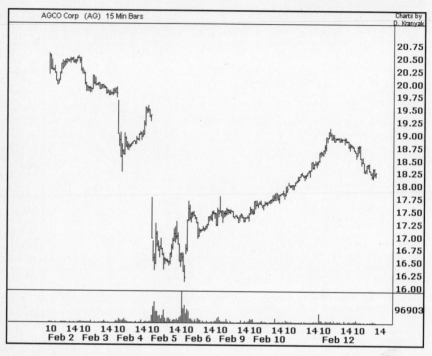

Figure 4.10 *(Continued)*

an abnormal, sudden aberrant reaction . . . it moved 15 points in only 3 days on heavy volume—it has broken its pattern! Even though the stock may have risen in price, this is not a positive sign, but rather a danger signal that *must be heeded*!

It was Livermore's belief that if you had the patience to sit with the stock all during its rise, now after the one-day reversal pattern appears you must have the courage to do the right thing and acknowledge this danger signal. You must now consider selling the stock, because you have received a valid warning signal.

Break-Out from a Consolidating Base

Stocks sometimes take time to consolidate and build a base before continuing their movement. This base allows time for the stock to take a breather and a chance for the sales and earnings to catch up to the new

Figure 4.11 The Reversal Pivotal Points are really the beginning and end points of trend lines. They appear when the trend is reversing. This chart of the Nasdaq clearly shows a Reversal Pivotal Point at the arrow in November/December.

valuation of the stock. In many ways, it is similar to a long Continuation Pivotal Point in function, although the formation looks different, and it usually takes longer for the Consolidating Base to form.

When the Consolidating Base occurs, the same patience must be applied to the situation as required with the Continuation Pivot Point—don't anticipate—rather wait for the stock to tell you by its action which direction it is going to go.

A common pattern of a Consolidating Base is called the *saucer pattern*. This pattern shows a slow, often long-term consolidating bottom that forms a kind of extended gradual change in trend as it develops into full maturity. To recognize this pattern, the trader must see a clear arc with tight trading ranges at the nadir, or bottom, of the arc. A

Figure 4.12 The Reversal Pivotal Points are really the beginning and end points of trend lines. They appear when the trend is reversing. This chart on Best Buy shows a clear Pivotal Point in November/December.

good trader can easily see the three boxes in Figure 4.18 of Lucent Technologies. These boxes are really consolidations, each at a higher level.

As stated, the pattern here in Figure 4.19 is very similar to the Continuation Pivotal Points pattern, where the buyers and the sellers are about equal in power. The stock lags along, or languishes and consolidates, waiting for the next move. These extended consolidations often come at the end of long market declines or advances. But the key rule still applies: *do not anticipate the next move*—wait patiently for the market to tell you—to confirm the movement either up or down.

Figure 4.13 When Continuation Pivotal Points form, they give the trader a terrific opportunity to wait and see what is next in store for the stocks. The Continuation Pivotal Point for Merrill Lynch appears in August/September and goes on to climb higher.

Break-Out on New High (or Low)

Livermore was one of the first people to realize that stocks breaking out to new highs often took off from there and had astounding runs. Large profits can be derived from this simple fact. As stated by Livermore: Often in the stock market people do not see what is right under their noses.

The thing with Livermore's genius was that he observed things like Industry Group movement, Pivotal Points, and break-outs to new highs, and so was able to incorporate these factors into his trading system.

Although others may have observed the same or similar things, they did not necessarily use this information in their trading. In fact, you will find that most traders have no real consistent proven system.They often depend on tips, instincts, analysts, brokers, friends . . . even astrologers.

Figure 4.14   This chart shows Verisign with two Continuation Pivotal Points in November/February and June/December.

Livermore's logic was always simple and to the point. New highs or new low break-outs were always good news for Jesse Livermore. Why? For him, they meant that the stock had pushed through the overhead resistance or underlying support and was very likely now to advance.

The theory behind heeding this pattern was that Livermore had observed that people do not want to sell their stocks for a loss. So, if they missed selling on the high, which happened to the bulk of investors, they would sit with the stock through thick and thin and, when it rallied, if it did in fact rally, and proceeded to get back to the old high, they would dump their stock to recoup their losses. So, when the stock broke out to new ground above the old high this meant to Livermore that all that old overhanging stock was now cleared out of the way. This meant clear sailing ahead, in most cases. So, he was in effect buying the stock when the majority of people had sold theirs and when the stock was in position to make a new run.

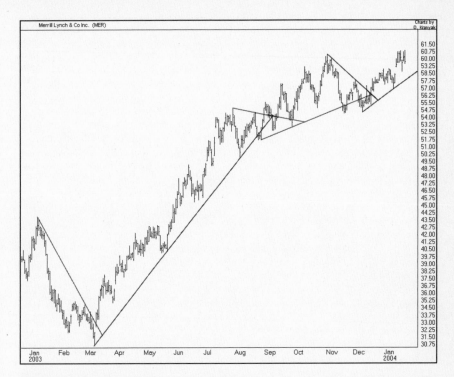

Figure 4.15 Merrill Lynch is a trending stock and can be fairly easily read and traded on its Pivotal Points.

Conversely on the short side, new lows mean people have given up on the stock and are now dumping it, throwing it overboard to get whatever they can for it. This often leads to a rapid fall into oblivion, or the stock proceeds to form a climax bottom, similar to the One-Day Reversal that we have already discussed, only on the downside. The stock will most often finally bottom out and form a Reversal Pivotal Point, and a new upward trend will begin at this juncture. At this point, the astute trader may want to reverse his position and move to a long trade.

Any trader will tell you that this sounds simple, but is difficult to do because the natural instinct is to buy cheap and sell dear. In this case, the Livermore Trading System instructs the trader to do the opposite and pay top dollar for a stock that has broken through the old high and now has a clear open field to run.

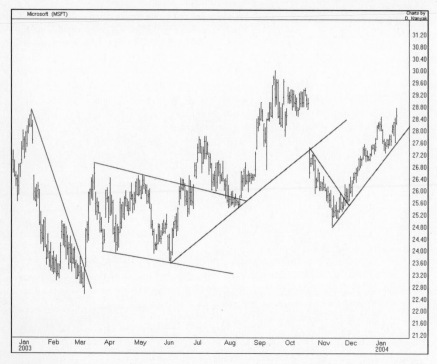

Figure 4.16   Microsoft is a choppy and confused stock with no trend or clear direction.

Figure 4.20 shows a New High Break-out Formation that appeared on a regular basis to Livermore in numerical form. Charts have been used for expediency.

Why these formations repeat themselves is unknown. Livermore attributed this repetition to human nature: "All through time, people have basically acted the same way in the stock market as a result of greed, fear, ignorance, and hope—that is why the formations and patterns recur on a constant basis. The patterns the trader observes are simply the reflections of human emotional behavior."

IMPORTANCE OF VOLUME

From the beginning of his trading career, Livermore was keenly aware of the importance of volume. Volume is a key factor in recognizing true Piv-

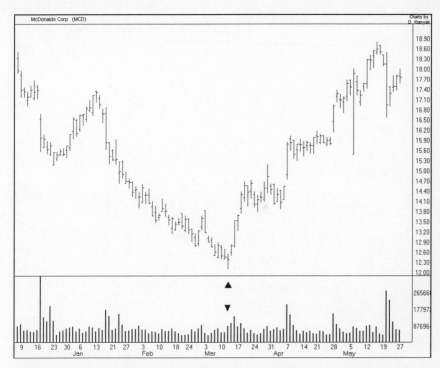

Figure 4.17   A One-Day Reversal occurs when the high of the day is higher than the high of the previous day, but the close of the day is below the close of the previous day, and the volume of the current day is higher than the volume of the previous day.

otal Points and other recurring patterns. It was obvious to Livermore that as the volume drastically changed in a stock, it was a clear *aberration* or *deviation* from the normal behavior of the stock. But was the volume accumulation or was it distribution? Livermore was an expert at detecting distribution. He had formed a strong opinion on that subject, because he knew how stocks were distributed by the pool runners of his day. The pool runners, experts like Livermore, were often charged with distributing the stock of the insiders who had formed a pool with their own stock for the purpose of controled distribution.

How did the pool runners do it? The same way as they do it today. Stocks were never distributed on the way up . . . they were distributed on the way down. The reasoning was simple—people will not take their losses when they should. The public will hold on to their stock as it drops and wait until it rallies back to the price where they bought it, so they can

Figure 4.18 A common pattern of a consolidating base is called the saucer pattern. This pattern shows a slow, often long-term consolidating bottom that forms a kind of extended gradual change in trend as it forms to full maturity. To recognize this pattern, the trader must see a clear arc with tight trading ranges at the nadir, or bottom of the arc. A good trader can easily see the three boxes in this chart of Lucent Technologies. These boxes are really consolidations, each at a higher level.

sell it. This is why so many stocks falter as they rally back to the old high. The people who bought at the high are now selling to get their money back—because they got a serious fright—and are now happy to recoup their losses.

To the astute trader, a change in volume is an alert signal. It almost always means that there is something afoot, a change, a difference, a possible aberration. A serious change in volume always caught Livermore's attention. He would ask himself—was it the volume leading to the blow off, setting the stage for a decline, or was it a real interest in the stock, was it being accumulated getting ready to be driven higher?

Figure 4.19 The Continuation Pivotal Point pattern occurs when the buyers and the sellers are about equal in power so the stock lags along, or languishes and consolidates waiting for the next move. These long consolidations often come at the end of long market declines or advances. But the key rule still applies: *do not anticipate* the next move—wait patiently for the market to tell you—to confirm the movement either up or down. Don't worry about clipping every point, wait for the insurance of having the market tell you what to do next. It is an important part of the Livermore Trading System.

Livermore never spent any time looking for the reason why the stock was attracting a lot of volume. He simply took it as an axiom that volume was an alert signal. It was happening, that *why* was enough for him. He knew that the actual reasons *why* would be revealed later when the chance to make money was gone.

Conversely, if there is heavy volume, but the prices stall and do not go up and make new highs, and there is no strong continuation of the current move, beware. This is often a strong clue, a warning, that the stock may have topped out and the accumulation is over and the stock is now going through a distribution phase.

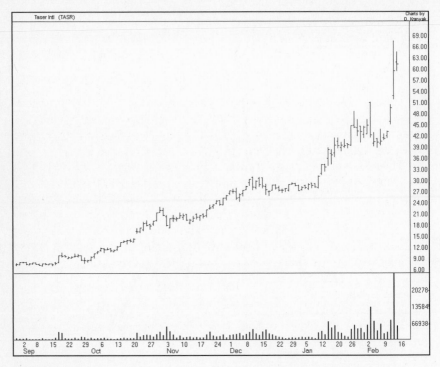

Figure 4.20 A break-out to a new high. One of Livermore's most bullish patterns.

Note: The end of a market move is usually pure distribution, as stocks go from strong hands into weak hands, from the professionals to the public, from accumulation to distribution. It is often a market move by the promoters of the stock, a deception, to trick the public, who view this heavy volume as the mark of a vibrant, healthy market going through a normal correction, not a top or a bottom.

This last gasp of heavy volume also provides a great opportunity to sell out any illiquid or large holdings. Livermore knew it was foolish to ever try to catch the tops or the bottoms of the moves. It is always better to sell large holdings into an advancing strong market when there is plenty of volume. The same is true on the short side, you are best to cover the short position after a steep fast decline.

Livermore was always on the alert for volume indications as key signals at the end of a major move, either in the entire market itself or in an individual stock. Also, he observed that at the end of a long move, it was not uncommon for stocks to suddenly spike up in a straight shot with heavy volume and then stop and roll at the top, exhausted. Then they would retreat, downward—never to make a new high before the on-slaught of a major correction.

As discussed before, there are two main trading systems available to the trader. The first is for those who believe that the stock market is a well designed rational, logical arena, for buyers and sellers to meet who buy and sell on what they feel is the *fundamental* value of a stock. These traders or investors believe that the stock market price is reflective of such things as a company's earnings performance, cash flow, balance sheet, and factory capacity, as well as future marketing prospects—earnings and sales.

These *fundamentalists* try and factor in the myriad reasons why a stock should earn more or less and therefore predict that the price will go higher or perhaps lower in the future—because it reflects the stock's earnings potential and overall performance. Put simply, these types of traders and investors believe the stock market is an orderly place and the price of a stock is based on logical deductive reasoning. If the market moves against them, they simply conclude that they have misanalyzed the situation or not accounted for all the factors in a proper manner.

The other group, which included Jesse Livermore, believed that the stock market is made up of human beings subject to human frailties. Livermore believed that most human behavior in the stock market was based on emotions, not logic, and people mostly acted in the market out of emotions rather than considered and deliberated reason. Therefore, he believed that a trader had to capitalize on the emotionalism of the market and ride along with that tide, not fight against it or try to explain it.

This theory is commonly called technical analysis, which involves the use of charts, pattern recognition, or mathematical algorithms to try and forecast the future price direction of the stock market as well as individual stocks. A major factor in technical analysis is the belief that all the major factors that influence the price of a stock, the basic information such as political events, natural disasters, personnel shake ups, earnings reports, and other psychological factors are absorbed and quickly discounted in the actions of the actual market itself.

Stated differently, Livermore believed the effect of all these external factors will show up quickly in the action of stock itself, primarily in the price movement. Therefore, the answer will appear in the chart itself. So, the trader should concern himself with what *is happening* not trying to predict what will happen!

Stock prices are determined in a way similar to an open auction, in which an item is worth whatever a person is willing to pay for it at that time. This is not an easy concept for most people to grasp. How can a stock be worth $20 at noon and $15 at two o'clock? After all, it's the same stock. The trader soon learns in the stock market that a stock is worth what a buyer will pay for it at any given moment.

One of Livermore's favorite books was: *Extraordinary Popular Delusions and the Madness of Crowds* by Charles Mackay, first published in 1841. This book describes John Law and the Mississippi land bubble and the seventeenth-century tulip craze when a single tulip bulb sold for more than four oxen, eight pigs, twelve sheep, two hogsheads of wine, and much more. This was also a favorite book of Bernard Baruch, a fabulous stock trader and close friend of Livermore's who also was one of the few people that did well in the crash of 1929.

In the final analysis there are only two pieces of information that a trader should look at—the price (high, low, close) of a stock and the volume (amount of shares traded). Remember, at the end of a day of trading, everything boils down to only these two factors—price and volume. All of the emotion is gone, all the guesswork disappears. The key information is always available to all the traders at basically the same time, yet some traders make money while others lose. It was Livermore's belief that the answers were always present in this factual information. If they are not clearly discernable to the trader, he should refrain from trading until they are clear. Why a stock or the stock market itself acted as it did was usually too vast a subject to study, too complex for any person, computer, or system to analyze.

Many technical traders place little importance on volume—not so with Jesse Livermore. The study of volume was a key element to be carefully analyzed at critical moments of a stock's life and history.

Livermore believed that anyone who is inclined to speculate should look at speculation as a business and treat it as such—not regard it as a pure gamble. He was convinced that speculation is a business in itself, and those people engaging in that business should determine to learn and understand it to the best of their ability with all the informative data available through technology.

Livermore once said to a friend: "In the forty years which I have devoted to making speculation a successful business venture, I have discovered and still am discovering new rules to apply to that business."

CHAPTER 5

Perfecting Money Management

Money Management is one of the essential three pieces of the puzzle that fascinated Livermore: Timing, Money Management, and Emotional Control are the main headings of his trading system.

Livermore had five main rules in managing his money. He attempted over the years to explain his entire trading theory to his sons—Money Management was a big part of it. But the sons never responded to their father. They were not interested in the stock market.

The excerpt below is from *Jesse Livermore World's Greatest Stock Trader* by Richard Smitten, published by John Wiley & Sons, Inc.

> One day Livermore called his two sons into the library at "Evermore" on Long Island. He sat behind the massive desk and the two boys sat down in front of him. He leaned forward and took a wad of cash out of his pocket. He peeled off ten one dollar bills. He did this twice, then folded the bills and handed each boy a pack of ten ones.
>
> The boys sat looking at him, each holding their money. "Boys, always carry your money folded and in your left pocket. Go ahead do it. You can keep the money."
>
> The boys did as they were told and put the folded money in their left pockets. "You see, pickpockets always go for a person's wallet, which is usually in the back pocket. Or they will come up behind you and go for your right front pocket, because most people are right handed. You all right with this so far, boys?" he asked.
>
> The boys nodded.

He continued. "All right, that's why you keep your paper money folded in your left pocket. See, if a pickpocket gets into your left pocket, and he gets that close to your balls, you're going to know about it."

The boys looked at each other.

Their father continued. "Don't ever lose your cash boys—that's the moral of this story. Keep it close to your balls, and don't let anyone near it."

MONEY MANAGEMENT RULE 1: DON'T BUY YOUR ENTIRE POSITION ALL AT ONE TIME

He liked to call this his probe system. Don't lose money, don't lose your stake, don't lose your line. A speculator without cash is like a store owner with no inventory. Cash is your inventory, your lifeline, your best friend—without cash you're out of business. Don't lose your damn line!

Livermore felt that it is wrong and dangerous to establish your full stock position at only one price. Rather, you must first decide how many shares you want to trade. For example, if you want to purchase 1000 shares as the full final position do it this way:

Start with a 200-share purchase on the Pivotal Point—if the price goes up, buy an additional 200 shares, still within the Pivotal Point range. If it keeps rising, buy another 200 shares. Then see how it reacts—if it keeps on rising or corrects and then rises, you can go ahead and purchase the final 400 shares.

It is very important to note that each additional purchase must be made at a higher price. The same rules, of course, would apply to selling short, only each short sale would be at a lower price than the preceding one.

The basic logic is simple and concise: Each trade, as it is established toward the total 1000-share position, must always show the speculator a profit on his prior trades. The fact that each trade showed a profit is living proof, hard evidence, that your basic judgement is correct in the trade. The stock is going in the right direction—and that is all the proof you need. Conversely, if you lose money, then you know immediately that your judgment was wrong.

The tough psychological part for the inexperienced speculator is to pay more for each position. Why? Because everyone wants a bargain. It goes against human nature to pay more for each trade. People want to buy at the bottom and sell at the top.

The speculator may choose a different ratio for purchasing the stock than Livermore's ratio of 20 percent on the first purchase, 20 percent on the second purchase, 20 percent on the third purchase, and a final purchase of 40 percent. He could, for instance, purchase 30 percent as the first probe position, 30 percent as the second and 40 percent for the final probe position.

In summary, it is up to each individual speculator to decide the ratio that works best for him. Livermore simply outlined what worked best for him. The main money management rule is comprised of three factors:

1. Do not take your entire position all at once.
2. Wait for confirmation of your judgment—*pay more for each lot you buy—dollar average upward.*
3. At the beginning of each trade first establish in your mind the total, exact amount of shares you want to purchase if all goes well, or specify the amount of dollars you are willing to commit; do this before you begin the trade.

MONEY MANAGEMENT RULE 2: NEVER LOSE MORE THAN 10 PERCENT OF YOUR INVESTMENT

He called this his Bucket Shop rule because he learned it in the bucket shops as a young man, when he worked all his trades with 10 percent margin. In the bucket shops, if the price of the stock went down below your margin requirements you were automatically sold out. If the loss exceeded the 10 percent limit, you were sold out and lost your bet. The 10 percent loss rule became Livermore's most important rule for managing money. In some respects, it is also a key timing rule, since it often automatically sets the time to exit a trade—when you have lost 10 percent or more of your invested capital, you must exit the trade. Also, a trader must set a firm stop before opening a trade. The consequences of big losses are drastic—you must gain back 100 percent to cover a loss of 50 percent.

TABLE 5.1 Livermore Percentage Loss Table

Starting Position	Amount Lost	Remainder	%Loss	%to Recover Loss
$1000	$ 80	$920	8.0	8.7
	100	900	10.0	11.1
	200	800	20.0	25.0
	300	700	30.0	42.8
	400	600	40.0	66.6
	500	500	50.0	100.0

Also understand that when your broker calls and tells you he needs more money for a margin requirement on a stock that is declining, always tell him to sell out your position. When you buy a stock at 50 and it goes to 45, do not buy more in order to average out your price. The stock has not done what you predicted; that is enough of an indication that your judgment was faulty! Take your losses quickly and get out.

Remember, never meet a margin call, and never average losses.

Many times Livermore would close out a position before suffering a 10% loss. He did this simply because the stock was not acting right from the start. He told friends that often his instincts would whisper to him, " 'J.L., this stock has a malaise, it is a lagging dullard or just does not feel right,'and I would sell out my position in the beat of a bird's wing."

Perhaps this was the inner mind working, distilling numerical patterns and formations that he had seen thousands of times before, and sending subconscious signals to his brain, unconsciously registering repeating patterns to be stored in his memory bank. Perhaps these patterns were subliminally remembered and awakened when recognized. Whatever it was, he learned over the years, through many of his market experiences, to respect these instincts.

He had observed countless times that people often become "involuntary investors." They buy a stock that goes down, and they refuse to sell and take their loss. They prefer to hold on to the stock in the hope that it will rally eventually and climb back up. This is why the 10% rule is essential. Livermore's advice: *Don't ever become an involuntary investor.* Take your losses quickly! Easy to say, hard to do.

If he bought a stock with a certain scenario in mind for what he expected the stock to do and it did not follow through with the expected scenario and go up immediately, he often just went ahead and dumped it, sold it automatically. He also never looked back—he had no self-recriminations after a bad trade or bitter thoughts if the stock later took off. He did, however, often study the trade to see what he had done wrong.

MONEY MANAGEMENT RULE 3: ALWAYS KEEP A CASH RESERVE

The successful speculator must always have cash in reserve, like a good general who keeps troops in reserve for exactly the right moment, when the odds are in his favor, and then moves with great conviction, and commits his reserve armies for the final crushing victory.

There is a never-ending stream of opportunities in the stock market. If you miss a good opportunity, wait a little while, be patient, and another one will come along.

Livermore used the analogy of playing cards—for him it was high-stakes poker and bridge. He believed it was only human nature to want to play every hand. This desire to *always be in the game*, is a common flaw and one of the speculator's greatest enemies in managing his money. It will eventually bring about disaster, as it had brought bankruptcy and financial disaster to Livermore several times in his early career. The observation made below is a critical factor in understanding the Livermore trading system.

There are times when playing the stock market that your money should be inactive, waiting on the sidelines in cash to come into play in the stock market. It was Livermore's belief that in the stock market:

Time is not money
Time is time
And money is money.

Often money that is just sitting can later be moved into the right situation at the right time and make a vast fortune—patience, patience, patience is the key to success—not speed. Time is a cunning trader's best friend if he uses it right.

MONEY MANAGEMENT RULE 4: YOU NEED A GOOD REASON TO BUY A STOCK AND YOU NEED A GOOD REASON TO SELL

Stick with the winners—as long as the stock is acting right, do not be in a hurry to take a profit. You must know you are right in your basic judgment, or you would have no profit at all. If there is nothing basically negative, well then, let it ride! It may grow into a very large profit. As long as the action of the overall market and the stock does not give you cause to worry, let it ride—have the courage of your convictions. Stay with it!

When you are in profit on a trade, you never need to be nervous. Livermore could have a line of a hundred thousand shares out on a single stock play and sleep like a baby. Why? Because he was in profit on that trade. He was simply *using the track's money—the stock market's money.* His attitude was that if he lost all his profit—well then he had lost money he never had in the first place, since he did not count the money as profit until he sold the stock and converted it to cash.

Profits Take Care of Themselves—Losses Never Do

Never confuse this approach of letting the position ride with the "buy and hold forever" strategy. How can any trader know what will occur far into the future? Things change: Life changes, relationships change, health changes, seasons change, your children change, your lover changes, why shouldn't the basic conditions that originally caused you to buy a stock change? To buy and hold blindly on the basis that it is a great company, or a strong industry, or that the economy's generally healthy was to Livermore the equivalent of stock-market suicide. He said: "There are no good stocks—there are only stocks that make you money."

As already discussed, one of the most important points in buying a stock was to try and buy as closely as possible to the Pivotal Point or the Continuation Pivotal Point. It was from this point that the key decisions are made. If the stock advanced from the Pivotal Points, you can hold it and relax, because from then on you are playing with the house's money, not your own capital. If the stock pulls away from the Pivotal Point in the opposite direction of the purchase, the experienced trader knows to automatically sell his position. It therefore becomes the trader's biggest job to find the Reversal Pivotal Points and Continuation Pivotal Points. This is the constant money management rule you must never break: cut your losses, let your profits run.

Stick with the winners—let them ride until you have a clear reason to sell.

MONEY MANAGEMENT RULE 5: PUT HALF THE PROFIT FROM A WINDFALL TRADE IN THE BANK

Livermore recommended parking 50 percent of your profits from a successful trade, especially where you doubled your original capital. Set this money aside, take it out of the stock market so you have to make a conscious effort to put it back in. Put it in the bank, hold it in reserve, lock it up in a safe deposit box, stuff it in your mattress—just put it somewhere safe. Like winning in the casino, it's a good idea, now and then, to take your winnings off the table, and turn them into cash. There is no better time then after a large win on a stock. Cash is your secret bullet in the chamber.

The single largest regret I have ever had in my financial life
was not paying enough attention to this rule.

—Jesse Livermore

Here is a summary of Jesse Livermore's money management rules:

1. Use probes—don't buy your entire position all at one time;
2. Never lose more than 10 percent of your investment;
3. Always keep a cash reserve;
4. You need a reason to buy a stock and you need a reason to sell;
5. Put half the profit from a windfall trade in the bank.

ADDITIONAL ADVICE

Stay Away from Cheap Stocks

One of the greatest mistakes that even experienced investors make is buying cheap securities just because they are selling at a low price. Although in some instances stock demand may push the stock from a small per-share price of say, $5 or $10 a share to over $100, many of these low-priced stocks later sink into oblivion by going into receivership, or else they struggle for years and years, with only the slightest prospect of ever returning a profit to their shareholders.

In selecting securities, it is essential for an investor to determine which industries or groups are in the strongest position, which are less strong, and which groups are comparatively weak, very weak, etc. The speculator should not plunge into cheap stocks in depressed industry groups just because the stock may appear to be a bargain. Stay with the powerful, healthy Industry Groups.

Keep Your Funds Liquid and Working for You

Perhaps nothing has contributed to the traditional poor success of the public in the investment markets as much as this fact—the average market investor does not keep his investment and speculative funds in proper circulation. The public is usually in a permanent loaded-up or tied-up condition, buried in a stock or a number of stocks with no cash or buying power held in reserve.

If the public observes a certain stock that may advance a few points a month, are they interested? No, they want something that moves more quickly. Yet in a few months they will probably wake up to see the stocks they refused to buy now selling for 20 points higher, while their cheap, volatile stocks, which they actually purchased, are selling at less than the prices they paid for them.

Disregard the Action of Insiders

Never pay any attention to the actions of insiders—this includes company directors and management. Insiders are commonly the absolute worst judges of their own stock. They usually know too much about their stocks, and they are too close to observe the weaknesses. Key executives also are usually ignorant about the stock market, especially market technical indicators and group movement. They are often reluctant to admit that the stock market is a specialty business and is an entirely different business from their own. In other words, you can be an expert in radio broadcasting or selling automobiles, or the manufacture of steel or pharmaceuticals, and most likely not know anything about trading stocks, especially in a volatile stock market as we had in the late 1990s and early in the new millennium.

Disregard Any Statement Made by Key Executives

The chief executive officer of most companies is little more than a cheerleader who has only one job with regard to the market. He must assure and reassure the shareholders, including the mutual funds and potential future shareholders, that everything is fine—if sales are down, he tells the shareholders that the decline is nothing more than a slight problem due to some temporary reason like seasonality, terrorism or competitors' lowering their prices. If profits are down, he assures the shareholders there is nothing to worry about, since the company has already reacted and made adequate plans to recapture their profitability.

Before Buying a Stock Establish Profit Target— Risk/Reward Ratio

The intelligent trader pays a lot of attention to the ratio of potential profit and the size of his overall investment. If a stock was trading at $200 and you are expecting a 20-point move or 10%, then you know you will have to put up $200,000 to make $20,000. This was not appealing for Livermore, because for him the risk/reward ratio was out of balance. No matter how good a trader you are, stock market losses are inevitable and must be considered as part of a trader's operating expenses, along with interest, brokerage fees, and capital gains tax. Few stock traders establish a risk/reward ratio before they enter a trade. It is essential to try to do this in order to have a specific money management plan.

Livermore was a lot less active in his trading than people thought. In fact, in his later life he was only interested in the "essential move," the important swing in the stock price. This often took extra patience in waiting for all the factors to come together to a focal point, where he felt as much as possible that everything was in his favor: the direction of the overall market, the industry group, the sister stock activity and, finally, an important Pivotal Point.

A famous misunderstood quote of Livermore was: "It was the sittin' and the waitin' that made me the money."

He did not mean the sitting and waiting *after* the stock was purchased—he meant *before* he pulled the trigger—that's when the trader must have the patience to sit and wait for all factors to come together to merge into the perfect trade, or as perfect as possible.

Remember, it is very difficult to work your way back from a devastating loss—this is true no matter what anyone tells you. Don't wind up without cash, like the merchant with no inventory—that's the same as a stock trader with no cash—out of business.

Always Establish a Stop before Making a Trade

When you purchase a stock, you should always have a clear price target of where to sell if the stock moves against you. And you must obey your rules! Never sustain a loss of more than 10% of your invested capital. Losses are twice as expensive to make up, as previously explained. This point can not be made often enough.

Always establish your stop before making the trade. This is another reason for buying on the Pivotal Point—it always gives the trader a clear point of reference. The Pivotal Point acts as a place to establish the *stop loss point*—the spot for the trader to close out the trade if things go against him.

Before making a trade, most stock traders do not take the time to observe the following rules:

- Decide on the potential of the trade versus the size of the investment—if it is a large investment with a small potential return, then pass. The trader should see a clear profit potential.
- Before you buy, make sure that you are buying at a crucial Pivotal Point, and use this as the spot to establish your exit point—your stop loss point if the trade goes bad. Write this number down and honor it—cut your losses—this is the most important thing for the trader to know, even if you get whipsawed and it rallies right back. It did not do what you expected it to do at the time you pulled the trigger–this is the most important thing to remember.
- Make sure all things are in your favor, market direction, group direction, sister stock direction and the exact timing is in place.

- At this point, the trader must then assume the status of an automaton, a robot, and he must then follow his rules.

Remember that no trader's judgement is infallible; if it were always correct, that person would soon be the richest on this planet. But it is not the case—we all make mistakes, and we will continue to make mistakes in our lives and in the stock market! The rewards can be enormous if we can learn to "cut the losses quickly and let the profits ride."

Points Are a Key to Money Management

Livermore wanted at least the opportunity of a 10 point gain in any stock he invested in.

Potential profit points were key in his trading. He was well aware that if a stock goes from $10 to $20 it is a 100 percent gain, whereas a stock that goes from $100 to $200 is a hundred point gain, as well as a hundred percent increase in value.

He always bought in round lots and used his probing technique to buy:

1. An initial position of 20 percent,
2. A second position of 20 percent,
3. A third at position of 20 percent, and
4. A final purchase of 40 percent, with all purchases being at a higher price and therefore higher cost.

This proved to him that the stock was moving in the direction he wanted it to.

As previously explained, the main challenge for the trader is to identify the current market leaders and to spot the new market leaders who are waiting to take over from the current ones. During major shifts and changes in market direction, it is of paramount importance for the trader to observe the leaders that are being driven out and identify the new stocks that will assume leadership in the future.

It is usually always best to go with the strongest stock in the strongest group—do not look for the cheapest or the laggard stock that has not yet had his turn to move in the group—always go for the strongest most dominant stock in the group.

Livermore's Method of Pyramiding

The trader must learn: *You never average down.*

That is, if the stock you bought goes down in price—*do not buy any more and try to average your price*—it hardly ever works. But what does often work is *"averaging up"* in *price—buying more as the stock goes up in price.* But this can be dangerous also, so try to establish your main position at the beginning, at the initial Pivotal Point, and then increase it at the Continuation Pivotal Point—providing the stock comes out of the consolidation with strength. The trader must wait until the stock has proven it is going to break out on the strong side of the Continuation Pivotal Point; until the stock declares itself, it is always a risk. At these junctures the trader must watch like a hawk and stay poised, but not biased by hope.

The final time a trader can pyramid is when a stock breaks out to a clear new high, especially if it moves on heavy volume (see Figure 5.1); this is a very good sign because it most likely means that there is no more overhanging stock to stop the progress of the stock for a while.

All pyramiding in the stock market is a dangerous activity, and anyone who tries it must be very agile and experienced, for the further a stock moves in its rise or decline the more dangerous the situation becomes. To

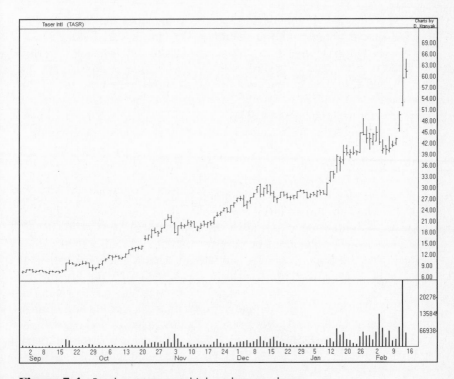

Figure 5.1 Break-out to a new high on heavy volume.

offset the risk, Livermore tried to restrict any serious pyramiding to the beginning of the move. He found it unwise to enter a pyramiding action if the stock was far from the Pivotal Point base—better to wait for the next Continuation Pivotal Point or the break-out to a new high.

The trader must always remember there are no ironclad rules to the stock market, the main objective for the stock speculator is to try and place as many factors in his favor as he can. And even with these in place, the trader will still be wrong on many occasions, and he must react by cutting his losses.

Here is a money management rule that cannot be stated often enough: A trader should always keep some cash in reserve for those incredible moments in trading the market when all the factors come together to form the "Supreme Trade at the Perfect Moment" such as occur at the zenith of bull markets and the nadir of panics. Many of these trading moments have recently occurred in 2003, and more still remain for 2004. There is no better feeling than having a strong army of cash standing by, waiting for your command to move into action.

Profits: The Spine of Every Stock

There is no magic about achieving success in the stock market. The only way for anyone to succeed in investments is to investigate before investing; to look before he leaps; to stick to the fundamentals of his own personal list of rules, and disregard everything else. But, of course, first he must establish his list of trading rules. Jesse Livermore was one of the most successful traders in history. In this section, the trader is getting a look at his money management rules.

Livermore would say to today's trader: "Take my rules and try them. I established them after having made many mistakes and thousands of hours of analysis and they work. If I can save you the pain and expense I endured, I will be happy to have done so."

Every trader must also understand that, in the end, in the final analysis, when the dust settles on a stock, it is the earnings—profits, and profit potential—that actually establish the final price of the stock. This happens when the emotions are wrung out and reality finally does settle in. But the trader must also understand that it is always hope and greed that grease the skids, lubricate the wheels of volatility on the stock's journey. The promise of superior earnings may have driven the stock in its history. But in the final analysis, it is real profits and real results that eventually cause the price of stocks to settle. Reality will always eventually set in to produce a final conclusion for the industry group and any particular stock. This will be revealed to the skilled technical trader as it occurs.

Don't Give Your Money to Others to Trade

It has become apparent in today's modern scandal-ridden markets that there is no security or safety in trading in the shares of large blue-chip companies or listening to highly accredited analysts, or trusting old, steadfast mutual funds. Where big money is concerned, there is always the danger of illegal activities lurking in the background. And there is no more money at stake than in the American stock markets.

The gangsters, the con men, the thieves, the swindlers, the grifters, all know where the money is and are always thinking of ways to help themselves to the stock trader's money. This comes as an additional burden in the field of stock trading, which is a most difficult field to begin with—a place where only the skillful, disciplined trader has a chance.

Here is one of Livermore's famous sayings: "If I am going to lose my money in the stock market, as so many people do . . . then I would prefer to lose it myself. I do not need a broker to lose it for me."

When you are handling surplus income, do not delegate the task to anyone. Whether you are dealing in millions or in thousands, the same principal lesson applies. It is your money. It will remain with you just so long as you guard it. Faulty speculation is one of the most certain ways of losing it.

Blunders by incompetent speculators and traders cover a wide scale. Livermore warns strongly against averaging losses. That is a most common practice. Great numbers of people will buy a stock, let us say at 50, and 2 or 3 days later if they can buy it at 47 they are seized with the urge to average down by buying another hundred shares, making an average price of 48 on all.

Having bought at 50 and being concerned over a three-point loss on a hundred shares, what rhyme or reason is there in adding another hundred shares and having the double worry when the price hits 44? At that point, there would be a $600 loss on the first hundred shares and a $300 loss on the second hundred shares.

If one is to apply such an unsound principle, he should keep on averaging by buying 200 shares at 44, then 400 at 41, 800 at 38, 1600 at 35, 3200 at 32, 6400 at 29, and so on. How many speculators could stand such pressure? Yet if the policy is sound, it should not be abandoned. Of course, abnormal moves such as the one indicated do not happen often. But it is just such abnormal moves against which the speculator must guard to avoid disaster.

So, at the risk of repetition and preaching, avoid averaging down. Livermore received one sure tip from a broker concerning a margin call: When the margin call reaches you, close your trade—never meet a margin call. This proves you are on the wrong side of the market. Why send good money after bad? Keep that good money for another day. Risk it on something more attractive than an obviously losing deal.

A successful businessman extends credit to various customers, but typically would not sell his entire output to one customer. The larger the number of customers, the more widely the risk is spread. Just so, a person engaged in the business of speculation should risk only a limited amount of capital on any one venture. As stated, cash to the speculator is like merchandise on the shelves of the merchant.

One major mistake of all speculators is the urge to enrich themselves in too short a time. Instead of taking 2 or 3 years to make 500 percent on their capital, they try to do it in 2 or 3 months. Now and then they succeed.

But do such daring traders keep it?

They do not. Why? They do not *take some money off the table from time to time.*

This one rule haunted Livermore because he did not always adhere to it. In fact, he consistently broke it. When he made a large profit in a trade, he did not take some of the profit off the table, out of the market and put it in the bank. It was one of the major regrets of his trading years.

Most people do not think they earned the money they make in the market because all they have done is make a phone call and shuffle some paper. There is no actual work involved in trading, no service being offered such as a doctor, mechanic, carpenter, plumber provides, nothing being manufactured like a lawn mower, a car, a suit of clothes. As a result, a lot of people have trouble psychologically, it appears to them as unhealthy money, rolling in rapidly, and stopping for but a short visit. The speculator in such instances loses his sense of balance. The uninitiated public investor says: "If I can make 500 percent on my capital in 2 months, think what I will do in the next 2! I will make a fortune with basically no work. I call, place my order with the broker, and collect my profits—it's no wonder rich people play the stock market."

Such speculators are never satisfied. They continue to shoot the works until somewhere a cog slips, something happens—something drastic, unforeseen, and devastating. At length comes that final margin call from the broker, the call that cannot be met, and this type of plunger goes out like a lamp. He may plead with the broker for a little more time, or if he is not too unfortunate, he may have saved a nest egg permitting a modest new start.

Businessmen opening a shop or a store would not expect to make over 25 percent on their investment the first year. But to people who enter the speculative field 25 percent is nothing. They are looking for 100 percent. And their calculations are faulty; they fail to make trading a business and run it on business principles. In the end, Livermore believed that the only money that is ever taken out of Wall Street by speculators is the money they draw out of their accounts after closing a successful trade.

Livermore used to tell this story to his friends:

"I recall one day in Palm Beach. I left New York with a fairly large short position open. A few days after my arrival in Palm Beach the market had a severe break. That was an opportunity to cash paper profits into real money—and I did.

"After the market closed I gave a message to the telegraph operator to tell the New York office to send immediately to my bank one million dollars to be deposited to my credit. The telegraph operator almost passed out. After sending the message, he asked if he might keep that slip. I inquired why.

"He said: I've been an operator here in Palm Beach for twenty years and that was the first message I ever sent asking a broker to deposit in a bank money for the account of a customer.

"He went on: I've seen thousands and thousands of messages passing over the wire from brokers demanding margins from customers. But never before one like yours. I want to show it to the boys."

The only time the average trader can draw money from his brokerage account is when he has no position open or when he has an excessive equity. He won't draw it out when the markets are going against him because he needs all his capital for margin.

He won't draw it out after closing a successful deal because he says to himself: "Next time I'll make twice as much."

Consequently most speculators rarely see the money. To them, the money is nothing real, nothing tangible. For years, after a successful deal was closed, Livermore made it a habit to draw out cash. He would draw it out of the market at the rate of $200,000 or $300,000 a clip. It had a psychological value for Livermore. He made it a policy to count the money over again. It was then that he knew he had something in his hand. He felt it. He spent a little. He knew his hard work was producing real money.

For Livermore, money in a broker's account or in a bank account was not the same as if you felt it in your own fingers once in a while. Then it meant something. There is a sense of possession that makes you just a little bit less inclined to take headstrong chances of losing your gains. So every trader should have a look at his real money once in a while, particularly between market deals.

Livermore was unable to make any money outside of Wall Street. In fact, he lost many millions of dollars, which he took from Wall Street and invested in other ventures, such as real estate in the Florida boom, oil wells, airplane manufacturing, and the perfecting and marketing of products based on new inventions. He always lost every cent.

In one of these outside ventures that had whipped up his enthusiasm, he sought to interest a friend of his in investing $50,000. His friend listened to his story very attentively. When Livermore finished, the friend said: "Livermore, you will never make a success in any business outside of your own. Now if you want $50,000 with which to speculate it is yours for the asking. But please trade stocks and stay away from business." The next morning, to his surprise, the mail brought a check for that amount, which Livermore did not need and sent back.

The lesson here again is that trading stocks is itself a specialty business like any other, and should be so viewed by all who wish to trade in the market. Do not permit yourself to be influenced by excitement, flattery, or temptation. Keep in mind that brokers sometimes innocently become the undoing of many traders. Brokers are in the business to make commissions. They cannot make commissions unless customers trade. The more trading, the more commissions. The speculator wants to trade, and the broker not only is willing, but too often encourages overtrading. The uninformed trader regards the broker as his friend and is soon overtrading.

Now if the speculator were smart enough to know at just which time he should overtrade, the practice would be justified. He may know of times when he could or should overtrade. But once acquiring the habit, very few traders are smart enough to stop. They are easily carried away emotionally, and they lose that peculiar sense of balance so essential to success. They never think of the day when they will be wrong. But that day always arrives. The easy money they might have made takes wing, and another trader goes broke.

Follow the rules—never make any trade unless you know you can do so with financial safety.

POSTSCRIPT

Many legends about Jesse Livermore have persisted over the years. In my research on Livermore, the following story was told to me by Patricia Livermore, his daughter-in-law, married to Jesse Jr., and then again by Paul Livermore, Jesse's younger son. I have written it down faithfully as it was told to me.

Livermore's Annual New Year's Ritual

"Good afternoon, Mr. Livermore."

"Hello, Alfred."

It was the Friday before the New Year of 1923. Livermore walked into the Chase Manhattan Bank, late in the afternoon. He was warmly greeted by Alfred Pierce, the bank manager. Livermore was one of the bank's best customers, keeping a balance of at least two million dollars in reserve for his special "stock situations," when he needed extra cash to establish one of his famous stock purchases or perhaps engage in a raid or activate a commodity corner.

"We have everything ready for you, J.L.," Alfred said. (People who knew Livermore well called him J.L.)

Livermore looked at his watch—it was almost 5:15. The bank was already closed. They had let him enter the bank through the employees' door. "Yes, J.L., the closing bank vault time-lock is set for 5:30, as always."

They walked in silence across the great vaulted room of the main branch through the door that separated the tellers' cages from the public and entered the back of the bank.

"And Monday morning?" Livermore asked.

"Monday, the timer on the vault is set to open at 8:00 sharp, like always."

"I just like to be sure." Livermore added with a smile.

"I understand, J.L.—by that time you will have had enough solitude."

"Yes Alfred, of that I am sure." Livermore said. He was carrying a leather briefcase. Alfred looked at the briefcase. "Do you mind me asking what's in the briefcase?"

"Not at all. It is my entire trading history for 1923. I will review every trade I made and refer to my notes. I keep good notes on all my trades that explain why I bought or went short and why I closed my positions."

"So you don't win every time?" Alfred said facetiously.

"Alfred, there are many rumors about me; of course, you know that I lose. I am only human. The idea is to get out fast when a trade goes against you. I often lose, that is what I am trying to figure out this weekend—why did I lose on certain trades over the year."

They approached the main vault. It was huge with a giant solid steel door. Two armed security men stood on either side of the door. They nodded at Alfred and Jesse Livermore. They knew what was going on.

The two men crossed over the threshold and entered the cavernous vault. There was a large amount of cash in a series of open chests. Most of the bills were hundreds with one chest full of twenties and fifties. There was a desk, a chair, a cot, and an easy chair in the middle of the cash. There was a special light above the desk and a second light above the easy chair. Livermore went over to the cash in the open chests and looked down at the uncovered bills. "There is almost fifty million here. The exact amount is written on the pad on your desk. The last of it came over from E. F. Hutton's this afternoon."

Jesse Livermore had sold out almost every position he had in both stocks and commodities, as he did at the beginning of every new year. He stared down at the cash.

"I would like to have the commission on just these sales, J.L.," Alfred said.

"This is not all of it. In some cases the market was too thin to take the hit, so that stock will be sold slowly over the next few weeks or so, and will be sent here for safekeeping."

"When will you resume trading?"

"Most likely in February, after I get to Palm Beach."

The red light on the ceiling started to flash and a low-level bell rang at 20-second intervals. The bank manager looked at his watch.

"Five minutes before the vault closes, J.L. The food is over here." The bank manager went to an icebox in the corner. "We got everything that your office manager Harry Dache ordered for you. He actually brought the food over himself about an hour ago, and we had an ice delivery around noon. Bread, cold cuts, vegetables, water, milk, juices and the makings for some old fashioneds." Alfred pointed into the open icebox door.

"Thanks, those old fashioneds will come in handy."

"Right you are, J.L. I'm going to leave now, I suffer from claustrophobia and all this money scares me."

Livermore walked the bank manager to the vault door. They shook hands. "J.L. if anyone ever knew about this . . . well . . . they might think that you were eccentric."

"Eccentric is a kind word, Alfred." Jesse Livermore smiled as the door started to swing shut, pushed by the two armed guards. "You see, Alfred, all year long all I see is and endless stream of paper. This weekend makes it real for me . . . real cash—nothing like it.

Livermore stood at the door as it clanged shut. The lights above the desk and the easy chair now provided an eerie but adequate light. Livermore surmised that no one had ever actually tested them with the door shut; no one would volunteer to be locked inside the vault.

He turned and walked to the desk surrounded by almost fifty million dollars in cash. For the next two days and three nights this would be his home. Inside the cavernous vault he would retreat into deep solitude and review his entire trading year from every aspect . . . just as he had done every year since he had started trading.

When it was time to leave on Monday morning he would go to the chest that held the twenties and the fifties and stuff his pockets with as much cash as he desired, and over the next two weeks he would spend it.

He had not locked himself up with his cash as a miser might lock himself up to count his money in the counting house. No, Livermore, because his world was a world of paper transactions all year long, believed that by the end of the year he had lost his perception of what the paper slips really represented—cash money, and ultimately, power.

By the end of the year, he was just shuffling paper. Livermore needed to touch the money and feel the power of cash. It also made him reappraise his stock and commodity positions and determine: Were these positions he would keep if he had the choice—were there better opportunities? Selling everything out forced him to appraise whether or not he would buy these positions back.

When he walked out of the vault on the Monday morning with pockets full of cash, he would start his shopping spree, a spree that usually lasted for at least a week and included spending on many human pleasures as well as material items.

CHAPTER 6

Emotional Control

The market is driven by psychological factors, not logic. A stock trader is caught in a maelstrom of thoughts and emotions once he has pulled the trigger on a trade. It is in this area that most of the grief occurs for the trader. So far, we have studied the Livermore Trading System's approach to timing and money management. We're left with this most important section—emotional control. Once we have made a trade, how do we control the myriad of emotions and thoughts that can easily cause us to make bad judgments and nullify all the other good work we have done up to the execution of the trade? No one is exempt from the emotional part of the trading equation with its pitfalls and dangers, including Jesse Livermore.

Livermore had an unquenchable thirst for knowledge about his chosen profession, and all his working life he was a constant student of the stock market. He was also a great student of the psychology of the market. At one point, he took psychology courses at night school in New York to better understand human nature. Livermore drew a conclusion from his studies: There may be millions of minds at work in the market, but there were basically only a few psychological patterns that had to be studied and understood—since human nature in market dealings is primarily driven by the common emotions of fear and greed, this leads to common traits of human behavior when buying and selling. In the stock market, this ultimately equates to common numerical and chart patterns. (See Figure 6.1.)

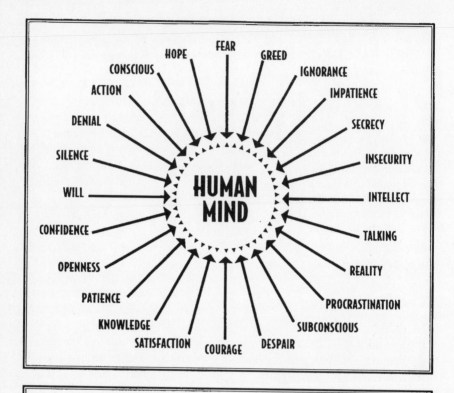

If we visualize the speculator at the center of the wheel, at the hub, we can see the emotional and psychological pressures that must be endured.

For Sigmund Freud, the human psyche is forever and inescapably in conflict by nature - a war that never ends.

For Carl Jung, the successful person ultimately seeks and achieves knowledge, enlightenment and harmony.

Each speculator must determine how they want to deal with their emotions and the psychological slings and arrows of the stock market.

Figure 6.1   An illustration of the Human Mind.

Later in his life he was asked an important question by his sons, Paul and Jesse, Jr.:

"Dad, why are you so good in the market and other people lose all their money?"

He said, "Well, boys, I have also lost money, but each time I lost, I tried to learn why I had lost. The stock market must be studied, not in a casual way, but in a deep, knowledgable way. It's my conclusion that most people pay more care and attention to the purchase of an appliance for their house, or to buying a car, than they do to the purchase of stocks. The stock market, with its allure of easy money and fast action, induces people into foolishness and the careless handling of their hard-earned money, like no other entity.

"You see, the purchase of a stock is simple, easily done by placing your buy order with a broker; later a phone call to sell completes the trade. If you profit from this transaction, it appears to be easy money with seemingly no work. You didn't have to get to work and labor for eight hours a day. It was simply a paper transaction, requiring what appears to be no labor. It gives the clear appearance of an easy way to get rich. Simply buy the stock at $10 and sell it later for more than $10. The more you trade, the more you made, that's how it appears.

"Simply put, it's ignorance."

The boys listened attentively, but they never had any interest in trading the market like their father.

A stock trader must constantly deal with emotions—when things go bad, there's often fear to deal with. Fear lies buried just beneath the surface of all normal human life. Fear, like violence, can suddenly appear in your life in the space of a single heartbeat, a fast breath, a blink of the eye, the grab of a hand, the noise of a gun. When it appears, natural survival tactics come alive, normal reasoning is distorted. Reasonable people act unreasonably when they are afraid. And people become afraid when they start to lose money; their judgment becomes impaired. This is our human nature in this stage of our evolution. It cannot be denied. It must be understood, particularly in trading the market. Sooner or later, fear will come to visit every stock trader who actively trades the market.

The unsuccessful investor or trader is usually best friends with hope—when it comes to the stock market, hope skips along the trader's path hand in hand with greed, but fear is always trailing along as well, hiding in the shadows.

Once a stock trade is entered, hope springs to life. It is human nature to be hopeful, to be positive, to hope for the best. Hope has been and will always be an important survival technique for the human race. But hope, like its stock market cousins ignorance, greed, and fear, distorts reason.

The trader must be acutely aware that the stock market only deals in facts, in reality, in cold numbers; the stock market is never wrong—traders are wrong. Similar to the spinning of a roulette wheel, the little black ball tells the final outcome—not greed, fear, or hope. The final result of stock market trading, which is posted in the newspaper at the end of every day, is objective and conclusive, with no appeal, like pure nature in the raw, a life and death struggle.

Livermore believed that the public wanted to be led, to be instructed, to be told what to do. They wanted reassurance. He believed that they would always move en masse, a mob, a herd, a group, because people want the safety of human company. They are afraid to stand alone because the belief is that it is safer to be included within the herd, not to be the lone calf standing on the desolate, dangerous wolf-patrolled prairie of contrary opinion—and the truth is that it usually is safer to go with the trend.

This is where it gets slightly complicated for most traders. Livermore was an independent thinker, yet he always wanted to trade along the *line of least resistance—the trend,* so he was generally moving along with the crowd, the herd, most of the time. It was when the *change in trend* started to appear, the change in overall market direction—that was the most difficult moment to catch and act upon.

He was always on the hunt for the clues to recognize a coming change in basic trend, looking for the Pivotal Point to form. A trader can never become complacent. Livermore was always alert, ready, prepared to separate himself from the popular thinking of the moment, the group thinking that usually always drives the market, and to go in the opposite direction.

Livermore believed in cycles. There is a time when things are good and a time when things turn bad. It is true in this life for all of us, and it is true in the stock market. The good times are coming and so are the bad times—the question for a successful trader is not *will* they come...it is *when* will they come? Livermore's conclusion—usually when you least expect it, the trend will change.

The change in trend is the most difficult time in a speculator's trading life. These major changes in trends were and remain hell. But Livermore knew these were the points where most of the money was lost, as was just experienced from 1999 to 2002. It is best to avoid the downhill slide of stocks, unless you have sold stocks short. There is always a way to make money in the stock market.

With this in mind, Livermore developed two rules:

First, do not be invested in the market all the time.   There are many times when you should be completely in cash, especially when you are unsure of the direction of the market and waiting for a confirmation of the next move. In Livermore's later life, whenever he deduced that a change was coming, and he wasn't sure exactly when or how severe the change might be, he cashed in all his positions and waited.

Second, it is the change in the major trend that hurts most speculators. They simply get caught invested in the wrong direction, on the wrong side of the market. To determine if you are right in your appraisal that a change in market trend may be coming use small position probes by placing small orders, either buy or sell, depending on the direction of the trend change you anticipate occurring. This will test the correctness of your judgment. By sending out exploratory orders and investing real money, you will get the signal that the trend is changing because each stock purchase will be at a cheaper price than the prior purchase—the signal—prices are dropping—time to go short.

The trader's job is to continually observe the tape and to interpret the tape as a person would look at a movie with no two frames exactly the same. No two markets are ever exactly the same, but they all have similar traits, like humans. These individual messages must be extracted from the tape and run through your brain in a rapid fashion.

The stock market always follows the line of least resistance until it meets with an at-first almost imperceptible force that slowly, but inexorably, stops its upward or downward momentum. It is at these key junctures—recognizing the Reversal Pivotal Points—being able to identify them and not be confused by natural reactions or the appearance of Continuation Pivotal Points—that the real money is made.

Just as the panics always encouraged Livermore to go long when things looked the bleakest, conversely, when everything looked perfect and blissful, it occurred to him that it might be time to go short. He tried to see this before everyone else did. That is why he kept his own counsel in silence and avoided, whenever possible, talking to anyone who might alter his thinking.

Sometimes, Livermore accumulated his line of stocks at what he believed to be the turning point in a great decline or at the crest of a mighty upward wave. He understood that it required time for general business to recover and for the earning power of these stocks to be reinstated, and so he was patient and prudent in assembling his line of stocks for either a new rally or in going short in a downward trading market.

He started trading at age 15 in the stock market. It was the focus of his life. He was very fortunate in calling the Crash of 1907 almost to the actual hour and very flattered when J. P. Morgan sent a special envoy to ask him to discontinue his short selling, which he did.

On his best single day during the Crash of 1907, he made $3 million. He was also prescient in his trading during the Crash of 1929 when he decided to go short with the market at its very zenith, he profited by $100 million.

But at first in the great collapse of the market in 1929, he went to the short side too early with the motors (car companies) as they rolled over—he lost over a quarter million dollars before he finally found the correct Reversal Pivotal Points as the key market leaders of the time rolled over and tumbled headlong into the great crash. He went short in earnest at that moment and increased all his positions. During the Crash of 1929, he made the largest amount of money he had made. He was blamed personally by the press and the public for the crash, which was pure nonsense. Nobody—no single person—could cause a market to do something that it did not want to do. Nevertheless, his life was threatened, and he was forced to protect his family with special security measures.

By 1929, Livermore had been trading for almost 40 years and had a finely developed intuition resulting from his enormous experience. But he later explained that, in retrospect, in all these cases the clues were evident in the actions of the stocks and spoke to him as clearly as can be imagined.

For Livermore, the people who invest in the market are akin to a large school of bait fish who have no specific leader, and they are capable of very quick, random action whenever they fear they are in danger. In other words, there are millions of minds involved in the stock market, these minds form decisions based on the two main emotions in the stock market, hope and fear. Hope is often generated by greed; fear is often generated by ignorance.

Livermore's main success emanated from his ability to find the main turning points, the Reversal Pivotal Points. In the long-term trends, this is the most crucial and important thing a stock trader must do. He was also convinced that if a trader, during the panics and the booms, was able to accurately find the perfect psychological moment (the pivot points) to exit and enter the market he could amass a fortune of great proportion. For a successful trader must be able to find and trade in the direction of the momentum—the direction of the line of least resistance. Livermore never had a problem in playing either side of the market (bull or bear, although he did not use these terms) because it was only logical to him, since he believed in cycles, that there were always going to be times to go long and times to also go short. The market goes up a third of the time, down a third, and sideways a third of the time.

If Livermore was exiting a long position, because he believed the stock has topped out, it was easy for him to consider getting on the short side of that same stock. He had no feelings for a stock, as some people do.

For instance, if a trader has made money with General Motors on the long side, the trader should have no emotional feelings for General Motors—the stock has simply done what the trader deduced it would do. If the trader can now make a profit as General Motors declines—by going short—he should do so with no feeling toward the stock, which is after all an inanimate thing with no feelings for the trader. There are no good stocks, nor are there any bad stocks; there are only stocks that make (or lose) money for the speculator.

Livermore had heard many of his fellow traders say: "That stock was good to me." Or "That stock cost me money, so I am staying away from it!" The stock had nothing to do with it. Everything that happens is a result of the trader's judgment and no excuses are acceptable. To put it simply, it is the trader or speculator who makes the conscious decision to enter a trade, and it is always the trader who makes the conscious decision to exit a trade. The judgment was either correct or it wasn't.

All traders must beware of a kind of arrogance, for when a stock moves against us we must decide that we were wrong and must exit that trade instantly. Most traders forget that it is a proven fact that we will always be wrong on some trades. It is getting out of those trades quickly that is the key to success.

Another trap the inexperienced trader must deal with is trying to find the exact bottom and top of a major trading cycle. Remember, there are times when a trader must be out of the market and waiting on the sidelines. It is virtually impossible to call the exact top and the bottom of any market, but it is much better to err on the side of caution. Getting out and waiting for the market to establish itself is very difficult while you are invested, because by being invested you will have an automatic bias toward the direction of your position. This bias stems from the hope. If you are long, you will subconsciously favor the long side, if you are short, you will subconsciously favor the downside. Hope lives in us all; remember, it is human nature to be hopeful. That is why Livermore often sold out all his positions and reevaluated the market from a cash position. It cost him the commissions, but he viewed this as a small insurance premium cost toward the overall profit goal. It is not what the millions of people think about the market, or say about the market . . . no, no, no, it is what they *do* about the market by their actual buying and selling; all this is immediately revealed on the tape; the problem is in the interpretation of this news, this evidence, as the tape flows past the reader.

This was Livermore's business, his life's vocation and the thing he most enjoyed. The work of solving the puzzle was what always fascinated him. It was never the money—it was solving the puzzle, the money was the reward for solving the puzzle. Going broke, which happened to him several times in his life, was the penalty for not solving the puzzle. The chief deception is that trading the market looks easy when it is one of the most difficult things to do—anticipate the trend. We must be aware of our emotional flaws and have the discipline to control and conquer the weaknesses of our human nature. It is the most difficult task a trader faces.

As Livermore explained to his sons: "I lost money when I broke my own rules—when I followed my rules, I made money."

HOW TO KEEP YOUR EMOTIONAL CONTROL IN DEALING WITH MEDIA NEWS

Livermore was always suspicious of everything he read in the newspaper and never accepted what he read at face value. He tried to look for hidden agendas and self-serving reasons that could have generated the articles, no matter what paper published the information. In Livermore's time, many news reporters were convicted of trading against the news they wrote about a stock. The reporters were also fed pure fiction, actual lies, by insiders to hype the stock.

He always tried to read between the lines and formulate his own judgment; that is why he often preferred to be alone, to formulate his own opinions and to use his own judgment when reading the newspapers. He did not seek the opinions of others in dealing with news releases. He tried to look below the surface.

Livermore told a friend: "I interpret these newspaper articles in two ways. First, I try to interpret their immediate and direct influence on the opinions and actions of stock traders with regard to a particular stock. Second, I watch the actual stock quotes to detect how the news has influenced the buying and selling of specific stocks as a whole in that market industry group. Often my interpretation of a news event is wrong. But I always know that if the news development is of sufficient importance it will eventually affect the tape.

"In other words, I watch the tape like a hawk to see how it is reacting to actual news. I do not listen to people, the pundits, the reporters, the analysts who are trying to interpret the news item and predict what will happen to a stock, an industry group, or the overall market.

"It is my experience that it is far better to look objectively at the tape, for the tape will provide the actual facts as to how the public is reacting to the news. These actual facts revealed by the tape are a far better indicator than any reporter or pundit can provide. It is up to the skillful market trader to watch the tape and react only to what the tape is saying. Learn how to read the tape—the truth is in the tape—listen to it. Try and avoid the opinions of so-called-experts."

One of the problems with looking too deeply into economic news is that it may plant 'suggestions' in your mind, and suggestions can be subliminal and dangerous to your emotional stock market health where you have to deal in reality, not supposition. These suggestions are very often logical, but that does not mean they are true and will necessarily affect the market. Logic does not drive the market. It is driven by human emotion.

CUT YOUR LOSSES, LET THE WINNERS RIDE

Note: This conversation and story are excerpted from *The Amazing Life of Jesse Livermore: World's Greatest Stock Trader* by Richard Smitten. The conversation, held at lunch, was between Jesse Livermore, Walter Chrysler (Chrysler Motors), Ed Kelley (head of United Fruit Co.), T. Coleman DuPont (DuPont Family), and Colonel Ed Bradley of Bradley's Casino in Palm Beach (Bradley was the owner of the longest running illegal gambling club in the United States).

"I've been hearing rumors on the Street about you and a wheat trade. Tell us about it, J.L., entertain us at lunch."

"Well, I just felt the demand for wheat in America was underestimated, and the price was going to rise. I waited for what I call my Pivotal Point and stepped in and bought 5 million bushels of wheat, about 7 million dollars worth.

"I watched the market closely after the purchase. It lagged. It was a dull market, but it never declined below where I bought it. Then one morning the market started upwards, and after a few days the rise consolidated, forming another of my Pivotal Points. It laid around in there for a little while, and then one day it popped out on the upside with heavy volume.

"A good signal, so I put in an order for another 5 million bushels. This order was filled at higher and higher prices. This was good news to me because it clearly indicated that the market line of least resistance was upward.

"I liked the fact that it was much more difficult to acquire the second lot of 5 million bushels. I then had filled out my predetermined target position of 10 million bushels, so I stepped back, and kept my eye on the market. It formed into a strong bull market and rose steadily for several months.

(Continued)

"When wheat rose 25 cents above my average price I cashed in. This was a bad mistake." Livermore paused as the lobster salads were served and the second bottle of champagne was opened.

Walter Chrysler asked, "J.L., how the hell could it be a bad mistake to make a profit of two and a half million dollars?"

"Because, Walter, I sat back and watched wheat rise another 20 cents in price in three days."

"I still don't get it," Chrysler said.

"Why was I afraid? Why did I sell? There was no good reason to sell the wheat. I simply wanted to take my profit."

"It still looks like a pretty good trade to me. I'm afraid you lost me, J.L.," Ed Kelley added.

"All right, let me explain. You remember that old joke about the guy who goes to the race track and bets on the daily double and wins, then takes all his winnings and bets it on the third race and wins. He does the same on all the other races, and wins. Then on the eighth and final race he takes his hundred thousand dollars in winnings and bets it all to win on a horse, and the horse loses."

"Yeah," Chrysler nodded.

"Well, he's walking out of the track and he meets a pal of his, who says. 'How'd you do today?'

" 'Not bad,' he answers, smiling, 'I lost two bucks.' "

They laughed. "That's a good story J.L., but how the hell does it apply to the wheat story?" Chrysler asked.

"Simple—why was I afraid of losing the track's money, my profits? In effect, I was simply acting out of fear. I was in too big a hurry to convert a paper profit into a cash profit. I had no other reason for selling out that wheat, except that I was afraid to lose the profit I had made."

"What's wrong with being afraid?" Dupont asked.

"So, what did you do, J.L.?" Kelley asked.

"Well, after I booked my profit in the wheat I realized I had made a great mistake. I had not had the courage to play the deal out to the end— 'til I got a signal to sell, a real definitive sell signal."

"So . . . ?"

"I re-entered the market and went back at an average price 25 cents higher than where I had sold out my entire original position. It rose another 30 cents, and then it gave a danger signal, a real strong danger signal. I sold out near the high of $2.06 a bushel. About a week later it sold off to $1.77 a bushel."

"Well, you have more guts than me, J.L., and it sounds a little like greed to me," Ed Kelley said.

"That's because you sell fruit, Ed. The way you know how to diagnose the market on fruit is the way I am supposed to know how to diagnose the stock and commodities markets, and the wheat futures market had shown no signs of weakness when I first sold it.

"The next time I sold the wheat it was different. I could see definite symptoms of weakness. It gave the clues, the hints, the tell-tale signs of topping out. The tape always gives plenty of warning time for the savvy speculator to heed."

"Well, J.L., I like your story but sometimes I think maybe you got a set of those lucky horseshoes up your ass, just like Ed Bradley here," Chrysler added.

"Well Walter, a little luck never hurt anyone." Livermore paused and looked around at the group. "I'd say we all had our share of luck at one time or another."

They all laughed.

THE WILL

Livermore agreed with his friend, the gambler, Colonel Ed Bradley—after *timing* and *money management* comes *emotions*. It is one thing to know what to do. It is quite another thing to have the will to actually do it. This is true of the stock market. This is true of life. Who knew better than Jesse Livermore?

Having the discipline to follow your rules is essential. Without specific, clear, and tested rules speculators do not have any real chance of success. Speculators without a plan are like a general without a strategy, and therefore without an actionable battle plan. Speculators without a single clear plan can only act randomly and they must react, to the "slings and arrows of stock market misfortune." This leads inevitably to the trader's defeat.

Playing the market is partly an art form, it is not just pure reason. If it were pure reason, then somebody would have figured it out long ago. That's why every speculator must analyze his own emotions to find out just what stress level he can endure. Every speculator is different; every human psyche is unique; every personality is unique and exclusive to an individual. Learn your own emotional limits before attempting to speculate. If you can't sleep at night because of your stock market position, then you have gone too far. If this is the case, then sell your position down to the sleeping level.

On the other hand, anyone who is intelligent, conscientious, and willing to put in the necessary time can be successful on Wall Street. As long as they realize the market is a business like any other business, they have a good chance to prosper.

Until this latest decline in the market starting in 1999, many people believed making money in the market was easy. Yet most Americans work, and anyone who works knows how hard it is to consistently make money in business, no matter what the business; it is never easy to make money. Livermore's friends all had their own businesses. He would never ask his good friends like Ed Kelly, the head of the United Fruit Company, to tell him the secrets of the fruit business or Walter Chrysler about the automotive business. It would just never occur to him. So, he could never understand when people asked him the question, over and over again: "How can I make some fast money in the stock market?"

He would smile and say to himself, "How could he possibly know how you could make money in the market?" He always evaded the question. He felt it was the same as asking him "How can I make some quick money in brain surgery? Or how can I make a few fast bucks defending some person in a murder case? He remained silent when asked because he believed that even attempting to answer these questions affects a person's emotions, because you have to take a firm position and actively defend your recommendations, which could change tomorrow, depending on the conditions of a dynamic stock market.

But he fully understood that he was not the only one who knew that the stock market is the world's biggest, most profitable gold mine, sitting at the foot of the island of Manhattan. A gold mine that opens its doors every day and invites any and all people in to plumb its depths and leave with wheelbarrows full of gold bars, if they can. And Livermore had done it many times.

The gold mine is there all right, and when the bell rings at the end of the day, someone has gone from pauper to prince, or from prince to supreme potentate .. or stony broke. And it's always there, the mountain of gold, waiting for the trader to pick up the phone and pull the trigger on a trade.

Livermore truly believed that uncontroled basic emotions were the true and deadly enemy of the speculator: Hope, fear, and greed are always present, sitting on the edge of a trader's psyche, waiting on the sidelines, waiting to jump into the action, plow into the game and mess things up.

This is one of the reasons he never used the words "bullish" or "bearish." These words were removed from his vocabulary because he believed they create an emotional mindset of a specific market direction in a trader's mind. Saying it's a bull market or a bear market causes the trader to believe that is the direction of the market. And there is a good chance the speculator will blindly follow that trend or direction for an extended period of time, even if the facts change.

Well-defined trends often do not last for extended periods of time. When people asked Livermore for a tip, he would say, the market is currently in an "upward trend" or a "downward trend" or a "sideways trend"—or tell them that the "line of least resistance is currently up—or down," as the case might be. That is all he would say and even that often got him in trouble with the public, because he wasn't around to tell them when the trend changed.

This strategy left him with the flexibility to change his mind, according to market behavior. He tried never to "predict" or "anticipate" the market, he only tried to "react" to what the market was telling him by its behavior.

Always be aware that when stocks decline swiftly, and abruptly, they are being driven by fear. When they rise, they are being driven by hope. That's why stocks go up slowly and fall rapidly. If people are hoping a stock will rise, they are slower to sell. If they fear the stock will decline, they are usually fast to dump that stock. That is why declines produce faster, more abrupt market action. So, if you play the short side you must be ready to react to faster, more drastic market patterns and conditions.

There is no good direction to trade, short or long, there is only the money-making way. To sell short often goes against human nature, which is basically optimistic and positive. In 2003, less than 4 percent of traders ever traded the short side of the stock market. There is also no question that it is *extremely dangerous* to sell short because the potential loss is unlimited. It takes strong control of your emotions to trade on the short side.

But the stock market moves up roughly a third of the time, sideways a third of the time, and downward a third of the time. If you only played the bull side of the market, you are out of the action, and your chance to make money, two-thirds of the time. And for good or bad, Livermore was not a man who wanted to wait, and hope, and wonder. He wanted to play the game, and he wanted to win more times than he lost.

Livermore was fully aware that, even in his time, of the millions of people who speculate in the stock market, few people spend full time involved in the art of speculation. Yet, as far as he was concerned, it was a full-time job, perhaps even more than a job, perhaps it is a vocation—where many are called and few are singled out for real success.

It is also interesting to observe that there are now, in 2004, more mutual funds than stocks on the NYSE. Most of these funds have strict charters demanding that they stay no less that 95 percent invested, with no more than 5 percent in cash. Also, in the charters of most mutual funds the managers of the funds can only go long in their trades. So, they have broken two of the Livermore rules–always keep a cash reserve, and always be ready to trade either long or short and also feel free to just sit in cash and wait for the perfect trade to appear. This is one of the reasons the hedge funds have done so well in the last few years.

BEWARE OF STOCKS TIPS

By far, the hardest emotional pitfall a speculator must deal with is tips. It was the main reason Livermore moved uptown to Fifth Avenue—to get out of the reach of everyone who was trying to help him by giving him sure things and inside information. Beware of all inside information and tips.

Below is an excerpt from the biography *Jesse Livermore—World's Greatest Stock Trader*.

Tips come from all sources. Once, long ago, one of these tips was passed on to me from the Chairman of a major American corporation who spoke to me at a dinner party at my house in Great Neck.

"How are things going?" I asked him.

"Great, we've turned the company around, not that it was really in trouble, but it looks like clear sailing from here. In fact, our quarterly earnings are coming out in a week and they are going to be terrific."

I liked him and believed him. So, the next morning I bought a thousand shares to test it out. The earnings came in just as the chief executive said they would. The stock rose nicely, the earnings continued to rise for the next three quarters, and the stock rose steadily. I was lulled into a feeling of security, as the stock continued to rise. Then it stopped and started plummeting in the opposite direction, like a waterfall.

I called the Chairman and said: "This fall in your stock price has me worried. What's going on?"

He answered,"I know the price has fallen, J.L., but we consider it nothing more than a natural correction—after all we have had a pretty damn steady rise in the price of the stock for almost a year now."

"How's business?" I asked.

"Well, our sales are slightly off and that news may have leaked out, I'm afraid. Looks like the bears got hold of that information and are hammering the stock. Its mostly short selling, a bear raid, we think. We'll drive them out on the next rally, squeeze them a little, eh J.L.?"

"Are you guys selling any of your holdings?" I asked.

"Absolutely not! Where would I put my money with more safety than my own company?"

Well, sure enough, I later found out that the *insiders* were busy selling into the stock's strength, the minute they got wind of the business going into a slump.

I never got mad. It was my stupidity and greed. I knew that all key executives were basically cheerleaders, and they must remain positive, must be bearers of only good news. They could never tell shareholders or competitors that things were not as rosy as they appeared. In fact, it always made me smile to listen to their mendacity. The misstatements, the lies, were just a matter of self-preservation, an essential part of the job of a chief executive officer—at every level of power, including politics.

But it was my self-preservation I was interested in, not the top executives and shareholders of the companies I invested in. Therefore after a while, and some substantial lost money, I never asked an insider again about how their business was doing.

Why waste my time listening to half-truths, shadowy statements, inaccurate projections, and just plain bold-faced lies when I could simply just look at the behavior of the stock? The story was clear in the action of the stock. The truth was in the tape for anyone and everyone to see.

I have suggested to people who were interested in the stock market that they carry around a small notebook, keep notes on interesting general market information and perhaps develop their own stock market trading strategy. I always suggested that the first thing they write down in their little notebooks was *Beware of inside information . . . all inside information!*

There is only one way to achieve success in speculation—through hard work, persistently hard work. If there is any easy money lying around, no one is going to try and give it to me—this I know. My satisfaction always came from beating the market, solving the puzzle. The money was the reward, but it was not the main reason I loved the market. The stock market is the greatest, most complex puzzle ever invented, and it pays the biggest jackpot.

(Continued)

And always remember: You can win a horse race, but you can't beat the races. You can win on a stock, but you cannot beat Wall Street all the time—nobody can.

People always talked about my instincts, especially after the Union Pacific story and the San Francisco earthquake. But I never thought my instincts were that special. The instincts of a seasoned speculator are really no different than the instincts of a farmer, like my father. In fact, I consider farmers the biggest gamblers in the world. Planting their crops every year, gambling on the price of wheat, corn, cotton, or soy beans, choosing the right crop to plant, gambling on the weather, and insects—the unpredictable demand for the crop—was more speculative. These same principles apply to all business. So, after 20, 30, 40 years, of growing wheat or corn or raising cattle or making automobiles or bicycles, the person naturally gets his sixth sense, his intuition, his experience-based hunches for his business. I consider myself no different.

The only area I may have differed from most speculators was when I felt I was truly right, dead right, for-damn-sure right—then I would go all the way, shoot the works. The way I did during the 1929 market crash when I had a line of one million shares of stock out on the short side, and every rise and fall of a single point meant a million dollars profit or loss to me. Even then, during my biggest play, it was never the money that drove me. It was the game, solving the puzzle, beating a game that confused and confounded the greatest minds in the history of mankind. For me, the passion, the challenge, the exhilaration, was in beating the game, a game that was a living dynamic riddle, a conundrum, to all the men and women who speculated on Wall Street.

Perhaps it was like combat is to a soldier. It's a mental high that's visceral, where all your senses are pushed to the limit and the stakes are very high.

"I told my boys—stay in the business you're good at." I was good at speculating. Over the years I took *many millions* of dollars out of Wall Street and invested them in Florida land, aircraft companies, oil wells, and new miracle products based on new inventions—they were all abject failures, disasters. I lost every cent I ever invested in them.

Just remember, without discipline, a clear strategy, and a concise plan, the speculator will fall into all the emotional pitfalls of the market and jump from one stock to another, hold a losing position too long, cutout of a winner too soon, and for no reason other than fear of losing the profit. Greed, fear, impatience, ignorance, and hope will all fight for mental dominance over the speculator. Then, after a few failures and catastrophes, the speculator may become demoralized, depressed, despondent, and abandon the market and the chance to make a fortune from what the market has to offer.

Develop your own strategy, discipline and approach to the market. I offer my suggestions as one who has traveled the road before you. Perhaps I can act as a guide for you and save you from falling into some of the pitfalls that befell me.

But in the end the decisions must be your own.

CHAPTER 7

How Livermore Prepared for His Day

*P*oise, *Patience*, and *Silence* are essential to achieve psychological balance.

Livermore believed that one of the most important qualifications for a successful trader was *poise* which, to him, was defined as stability, balance, and dignity of manner. A poised person is a person who can handle his hopes and fears in a calm way.

The other qualification is *patience*, to wait for the opportune time, when as many factors as possible are positioned in the trader's favor. Poise and patience are the close friends of successful traders.

The final qualification is *silence*. Keep your own silent counsel—keep your victories and your failures to yourself—learn from them both. Poise, patience, and silence are attributes that must be cultivated—these virtues do not come automatically to the stock market trader.

Livermore's early experiences working at 15 as a board boy in the Paine Webber office in Boston had a profound impression on him. He had no time for group behavior when trading stocks for his own account. His early observations had convinced him of the pitfalls of listening to other people. Even if you knew the rules, sometimes other peoples' opinions would sink subconsciously into your mind and influence your trading.

It was Livermore's opinion that a person's work space when trading the market was very important psychologically and could play a major role in the ability to trade. He also felt that the serious trader's trading space provided the largest part of their income, so he did not hesitate to spend money on his work space. He was quite aware that setting up a proper working environment could mean a great deal in profits on the trades he made. Livermore's office was his sacrosanct Trading Room.

His main objective was to protect himself from all unwelcome bad influences—in particular he was trying to avoid anyone who might be inclined to offer assistance by giving him some information in the form of a tip. Tips were the one thing that had done him the most harm in trading.

He never wanted to be part of a group of stock market traders, especially those who gathered in the brokerage offices. His main reason was that he needed focused continuity of thought for more than 15 minutes at a time. He had no interest in tips, gossip, and the interpretation of the daily news events concerning the stock market by the people gathered in an office.

The larger brokerage offices where great numbers of people gathered was chaos to his brain. As far as he was concerned, it was hurtful to his trading to be with these people, with their own individual biases and their own hidden agendas, which did not necessarily match up with his own. He believed in working in silence and keeping his own counsel. As a friend of his once told him, "I do not take tips. I prefer to make my own mistakes—not the mistakes of other people!" As far as Livermore was concerned, his friend was right.

He always traveled from his home to his offices undisturbed, either by car or on his yacht in the better weather. He did this in silence, carrying no other passengers; this gave him a chance to read the newspaper and plan his day. He did this to avoid meeting people who would inevitably inquire about the stock market; the subject came up almost automatically because Livermore was so famous. He would then be forced to listen to tips, gossip, and prognostications that would inevitably creep into his conscious and subconscious mind and therefore affecting his judgment. If he traveled by himself, he could continue his thoughts without any interference in implementing his plan for the day. He used to borrow his friend Bernard Baruch's method, who told his brokers: "If you know anything about the stock I am trading . . . please do not tell me."

Livermore was often the first one to the office, followed by Harry Dache, his office and security manager. The board men, usually six in total, arrived at the office by nine o'clock to take their positions on the chalkboard to file the trades as they occurred. For volume numbers, Livermore consulted the actual ticker tape. He positioned the main ticker in the center of the room on a tall podium so all he had to do was raise or lower his eyes from the tape to the chalkboard to see the action of stocks he owned or was interested in. He also employed telephone lines that went directly to the hot posts he was trading at the time, say, steel, motors, mail order, or radio.

He used the largest and fastest ticker tape and positioned it at near eye level, so it was easily accessible. In fact, he generally used tall ticker tapes so that he was forced to stand while reading the tape. Standing in an erect position ensured proper blood circulation and better breathing. He found this helped to keep him calm during stressful trading periods. He made it his policy to be on his feet nearly all the time that the market was open. This gave him a little exercise and kept his senses at a higher pitch. He was never bent over or lounging. He considered the market a great challenge that demanded total concentration—it was not for the lazy. He even stood while telephoning.

He allowed no talking once the bell rang; he demanded silence in the office while the market was open. His phone number was known to very few people, and he would often change it to keep people from reaching him. He received and answered as little mail as possible during the work day. He was only interested in the stock market; it was his sole job, and he considered everything else an unwelcome distraction.

One of the things he liked best about his job, after he had fallen into many pitfalls and managed to climb out, was the solitude—he loved the individuality, being the lone wolf—everything that happened occurred as a result of his judgment. He structured his office so there were as few outside influences as possible.

He had no interest in sharing his market experiences with anyone— the good or the bad. His attitude was "how could they care, or help me, my trading had nothing to do with their lives, and they certainly couldn't help me." Further, he wanted no help. He was also conscious of the fact by then that if you do well, if you are successful, most people become envious, and they covet your success; if you do poorly they revel in your misfortune and tell their friends that you have finally been humbled by the stock market—and that *You had it coming* for your reckless behavior. So silence is best, since there is nothing to gain through informing people of your activities. The satisfaction of *being correct*, understanding and beating the tape . . . it was enough for *him* to know. He did not have to tell other people of his successes or failures. By then, it was usually too late anyway, the trade was over.

On October 5, 1923, in order to fully practice his new techniques and theories, he moved his offices from 111 Broadway uptown to 780 Fifth Avenue, the Heckscher Building. He designed the offices very carefully. He wanted to be away from the Wall Street atmosphere, out of earshot of any tips. He also wanted to have more secrecy and security in his operations, so that no one could know his trades. Sometimes, he used over fifty brokers to downsize and spread out the orders in order to keep his trades secret.

Inside the building, there was a private express elevator that traveled only to Livermore's penthouse floor. The offices occupied the entire floor. He purposely had no sign on the office door where the elevator stopped. Once inside this door, there was a small anteroom, a kind of waiting room where Harry Edgar Dache had one of his desks.

Harry was described by the New York Press as pug ugly with a personality to match. He stood a solid six feet six inches and weighed close to 300 pounds with the battle-scarred face of a pugilist. Harry's looks belied his high intelligence. Livermore had interviewed him for only half an hour and hired him on the spot. Harry had been in the Merchant Marine and traveled the globe many times. He spoke six languages, including Latin. He was a voracious reader, knowledgable in many areas, and a terrific administrator. He ran the office with secrecy and perfection. He was completely loyal to Livermore and very protective of him and his family. The boys loved Harry. Jesse Jr. and Paul were enthralled with his magical stories of traveling the seven seas. He was their unofficial tutor, chauffeur, companion, and bodyguard, especially when they went to Palm Beach.

There were no windows in the anteroom, only a few chairs and Harry's desk. Behind Harry was the solid floor-to-ceiling door to the offices. There were no signs or identification on any doors. To let someone in to see Livermore, Harry would always confirm the appointment first by intercom, when the guest arrived, no matter who it was. He would then rise from his desk and use his key to open the door to the offices for the visitor. It was a theatrical ritual that Harry liked to perform, to show the visitor the difficulty in gaining entrance into the Trading Room. And it worked.

Behind the door was a massive open room with a green chalkboard that ran the entire length of the room. There was a catwalk in front of the chalkboard where four to six men would work in silence. They each would have a section of the board. They were responsible for active stocks or commodities being traded or stocks on the watch list that were being closely observed.

These men were paid very well and sworn to secrecy; Harry Dache assured they remained loyal. Each man wore head phones that connected to the floor of the exchange. Men on the floor would often call up the instant quotes to Livermore's board men, who would immediately write down the individual stock transaction—the bid, asked, and sold price. So, on many occasions, they did not work off the ticker tape. It was too slow. This gave Livermore an edge on the ticker tape, which was usually delayed at least fifteen minutes and up to hours in a fast market. He wanted the most current information he could get—he had learned the hard way as a young man how important fresh quotes were.

If Livermore was active in several stocks or commodities, he would often increase the staff from four to six men on the chalkboard. These men would work all day on the catwalk, in silence, only taking a short break for lunch, when they would usually be replaced by Harry, so no quotes were lost.

These board men would always track two or more stocks in the same group. If Livermore was trading General Motors, he would track Chrysler as well, to observe the Industry Group action.

In the middle of the office was a massive conference table of shiny mahogany with eight comfortable leather armchairs. On the rare occasions when guests were invited to the office, he would always sit facing the chalkboard so he could watch the quotes as he listened to the guests. Livermore would, on occasion, interrupt the meeting to enter his office and place his trades in private.

His personal, private office was very large, with heavy oak and mahogany paneling. He had seen the paneling in a library in an old English manor and had purchased it. The library was disassembled and shipped to New York where it was reassembled.

His desk was large, made out of highly polished mahogany. On the desk were an In basket and an Out basket, and a pad and pencil. The wall adjacent to the mahogany desk that faced the chalkboard was a solid sheet of clear plate-glass, so he could see the market action as it happened from his desk. The glass was cleaned personally by Harry at least once a week.

There were three black telephones on his desk. One was a direct wire to London, the second went to Paris, and the third went directly to the floor of the Chicago grain pits. He wanted first-hand, fresh information, and he was willing to pay for it. He knew that wars were won on information and intelligence, and the general with the best information, the best intelligence, was the one most likely to win. And he wanted no rumors of war, he wanted only specific, accurate information.

His son Paul often came to this office as he grew up, especially on his summer breaks. Livermore sometimes allowed him to work the chalkboard. The board men were trained to work with a code that they explained to Paul. If a stock suddenly had a deep price fluctuation, they would use a secret code to note this on the board. These codes were known only to the board men and Livermore. It was what he later called his *Livermore Secret Market Key*. On occasion, there would be guests in the office who would ask him: "J.L. what the hell are those weird columns on the chalkboard, some kind of hieroglyphics?"

"They make perfect sense to me," he would respond.

"You wanna explain them to me?"

"No," he would smile. "If I did, then you would be as smart as I am."

"Just tell me what to buy and sell—and when—that's all—keep it simple for me."

"You know I never recommend a stock, but I would be glad to tell you whether I believe the market is going up or down."

"It always goes up or down, J.L".

"You're right of course, but the trick is *when* is it going to go up or down."

"And *what* stocks are going to go up or down, J.L.? Don't forget it's what particular stocks are going to go up or down; that's what we all want to know—what stock will rise and when."

"If a man knows the general trend of the market he should be able to do well."

"Whatever you say, J.L., whatever you say."

One day he was sitting in his office talking to his son Paul, when he said, "Turn around Paul, and look at the chalkboard."

Paul turned and studied the men as they moved on the catwalk like well choreographed dancers.

Livermore continued: "You see, son, those markings on that board are as clear to me as a musical score is to a great conductor. I see these symbols as alive, a rhythm, a heartbeat, a pulse, that makes beautiful music—it all makes perfect sense to me. For me the board is alive, like music; we are able to communicate. It's something that has come to me only after years of hard work and practice, not unlike a great conductor of a great orchestra. What I feel when I look at that board can't be shared, anymore than a conductor could articulate what he feels when he plays Mozart just the way it should be played. The board and those men are a playing a symphony for me, a symphony of money—that sings to me—that makes love to me—that envelops me in its song."

Paul studied his father carefully that afternoon. He believed every word. It was a rare moment for Paul, to get so intimate with his father, who was a private man, stingy with his emotions, frugal with his love.

HOW LIVERMORE PREPARED FOR HIS DAY

Livermore developed the following rule from a great trader: Keep stress at bay—act in all ways to keep the mind clear and your judgment correct. Livermore did all he could to achieve this in his physical life by going to bed early, eating and drinking lightly, taking exercise, standing upright at the stock ticker, standing while on the telephone and demanding silence in the office. He made it a rule to speak to no one on his way to work and he kept silent about his stock market transactions.

Jesse Livermore was a highly disciplined man. During the week, he went to bed every night at 10:00 P.M. and arose each morning at 6:00. He preferred to have no one around him for the first hour. This early time was for him. It was the time, after sleep, when he was most alert and open to absorbing information. The kitchen staff was trained to leave his coffee and juice on the table in the solarium, if he was in his mansion at Great Neck, Long Island.

The newspapers were also laid out for him, including the European and Chicago newspapers. He read voraciously all his life. He wanted this hour or two to plan his day. Livermore had observed that few men really planned their day. Yes, they were organized, they had appointments scheduled and lunch engagements, and public affairs planned and written down. They often had secretaries to assist them. They knew in detail what awaited them, meetings, people coming by the office, phone calls they would make and receive. They knew what had been planned for them, but what items of major importance had they planned actually to get done for themselves, and did they prioritize their time?

Livermore, on special occasions, spoke to his two sons, Paul and Jesse Jr., of his business while in his massive library in the house on Long Island: "Boys, you will find that hardly any businessman really plans his day to handle the most important items. In most cases his day is laid out for him—organized for him by his secretary and his staff. He is merely an attending party. At the completion of the day he is often left with the most important matters still unattended, unexamined, uncompleted. Important strategy matters in running a complex business are perhaps not being attended: personnel problems, mergers and acquisitions, raising capital, and great marketing concepts—like buying on the installment plan was to banking—or perhaps the competition is not being clearly examined or assessed until it is too late.

"Not so for me. In the stock market my moves must be based as much on clear facts as they can be. To play the market properly requires silence, and seclusion to examine the situation, and to appraise, and deliberate on new information that comes to hand during the trading day. One must always have a clear strategy to play the market and clear rules to follow.

"I have found that it is easy to pick up the phone and pull the trigger by buying or selling. The problem is knowing when and what to do, and to follow religiously your own rules and discipline.

"Boys, I decided long ago in the stock market that if there are going to be mistakes made in my trading—I want them to be *my mistakes*. I don't need some one else to lose my money for me by giving me tips or influencing my trades. In the business I am in, there is no room for post mortems, you either make money or you lose money . . . or your money just sits there waiting for the right situation while earning small interest.

"That's why I go to bed at ten and rise at six. The careful, disciplined man must be aware of everything, ignorant of nothing. You cannot afford to be careless about anything. Sometimes overlooking a single item, big or small, can ruin everything, kill all your plans. Like a general in wartime—his men's lives depend on his thoroughness in planning and executing that plan. In the stock market there is no room for error and carelessness.

"People think that I am simply a speculator, a trader, who finds situations and plunges into them. Nothing could be further from the truth. I often pick up small, seemingly useless clues in the newspapers and after checking them out, investigating what is behind them, I will act upon them.

"You ask about my day? In the solitude of the morning hours, after being rejuvenated from sleep, with nothing to distract me, I carefully read the papers. I have often used small specific news items like weather events, like droughts, insect problems, labor strikes, and assess how they would affect the corn, wheat, or cotton yields that often lead me to a possible good trade.

"I got my real news on the financial side by examining the actual prices and actions in the commodities market such as coal, copper, steel, textiles, sugar, corn, wheat. I also looked at the automobile sales, and employment figures. I got a feel from this information and often a correct judgment on general business conditions in the United States. It was no one single fact, it was a plethora of facts that often led me finally down a narrow path to a trade.

"I did more than just scan the headlines of the newspaper; I read the paper carefully looking for small items of news that might provide me with important clues, especially about an Industry Group or a specific stock that had changed from weak to strong or vice-versa.

"The headlines are for the suckers. A good speculator has to get behind the news and see what was really going on. Beware, often misleading articles are planted by people or brokers with hidden agendas, who want to sell their stock on the good news or they want to keep people invested while they go ahead and distribute their own stock.

"Once I traveled in my railway car to Pittsburgh where I observed that the steel mills were not at 30 percent of capacity, they were at less than 20 percent and falling. In other words, the steel stocks were a perfect short sale.

"Unfortunately, many people who invest in the market only read the headlines, and they too easily believe what they read. This is not good, since there are many pitfalls, schemes, and dangers. Slick money traps always appear wherever great sums of money are involved, such as the stock market. It is my observation that often what you read in the newspaper is nothing more than another form of a planted stock tip—so the reader has to be aware of the source, motives, and effect of what he is reading on the stock market, otherwise chances are he or she will become a sucker too.

"Boys, it is my observation that there is no better time than the early morning to gain an enormous advantage toward being a successful stock trader. There is silence in the house, no person or thing is disturbing your concentration, and the mind is renewed after a good night's sleep.

"You will learn as you grow older that most people simply get up at a certain time in the morning, get ready, and go directly to the office. Often, these same people feel the desire to go out at night during the week to the cinema, a play, a long dinner with several drinks. In other words, they feel the need for social interaction or recreation during the weekdays. This may work well in other fields of endeavor, but it is a dangerous practice on a regular basis if a person wants to be successful in seriously trading the stock market. A good stock trader is not unlike a well-trained professional athlete who must keep the physical side of his life in perfect form if he wants to continue to be at the top of his mental form. The body must be in tune with the mind, for there is no more intense or exciting field of battle than the stock market. A person is making a mistake if he thinks success in the stock market comes easily, instantly, or steadily without great effort. The successful trader must always be in top physical form."

The boys always enjoyed their father's time with them, especially as they grew older. It was rare for him to spend a lot of time with his sons. His oldest son, Jesse Jr., lived a life full of strife and torment, until he finally took his own life in Palm Beach.

During the week, Livermore had always been willing to sacrifice the diversions offered to people from ten o'clock at night until two in the morning. He did not feel he had missed anything by being asleep during this period, and up at five or six in the morning. All Livermore's life, he found that there is true joy in the solitude and the pure mathematical work he did during this time. For he always believed he was in search of bigger game than just pleasure and social interaction. He wanted to be supreme in his endeavors in the stock market—this is what gave him the real pleasure and satisfaction: playing the game and winning the game.

It was his observation that the public sincerely believes that the stock market is an easy way to make money. If they have some extra money to invest, they believe the stock market should offer them an easy way to increase the value of that money.

This is not the case and never has been. Livermore observed that people who have no knowledge of the stock market, but insist on playing it, generally lose their money in a hurry.

In Livermore's view, if you want to succeed in the stock market, make sure you get plenty of sleep, give yourself plenty of time for the uninterrupted study of all the elements involved with the stock market, and remember that the key to success in the stock market is knowledge and patience. So few people succeed in the market, because they have no patience and are generally ignorant of the market. Finally, they want to get rich quickly.

Anyone who figures that his success is dependent upon chance may as well stay out of the market. His attitude is wrong from the very start. The great trouble with the average persons who buys securities is that they think the market is a gambling proposition.

One should realize at the outset that to work in the stock market requires the same study and preparation as law or medicine. Certain rules of the stock market are to be studied as closely as if you were a law student preparing for the bar. Many people attributed Livermore's success to luck. As Livermore said, "That is not true; the fact is that since I was 15, I have studied this subject closely. I have given my life to it, concentrating upon it and putting into it my very best."

SUMMARY OF LIVERMORE ADVICE

- Keep your own counsel;
- Maintain silence on matters concerning the stock market;
- Do not listen to or take tips.

If Jesse Livermore were still alive, he would advise the current traders of today: If you want to watch FNN or MSNBC or Bloomberg, then do so with the volume in the mute position.

It was Jesse Livermore's belief that you should never listen to a top company executive talk about his company. He is simply acting like a cheerleader. In order to keep his share price high or at least where it is currently trading, the corporate executive is often compelled to shade the truth. He believed that top executives often simply tell lies about their company's situation. The same may be true of the "impartial" analysts who secretly may hold stock or they may be ordered to give a favorable report by the company they work for. A trader can be duped by these sources.

The entire subject of the media is an area that can throw the trader off balance, since the media and their guests can present financial material any way they want. But it does not matter what people say. What matters is what the market says. Let's take an example: The head of the Federal Reserve Bank makes a statement at a speech given at a college one evening and the press picks up a few sentences out of the speech like "It is my desire that the country not enter a trade war with the European Common Market," and it comes out in headlines: "Greenspan Says We Are About to Be Engaged in a Trade War with the European Common Market—Expect New Embargoes and High Tariffs on American Goods Going to Europe."

The next day the market takes a severe drop at the beginning of trading. The smart trader will wait and stay calm because he knows this will pass and the market will most likely absorb the news and recover back to where it was. The answer lies in the action of the market—not what people say about things.

This of course, is a complicated issue since with sudden real news such as a war or a natural disaster, those items may affect the market on a real basis. And don't misunderstand please—Livermore kept up with current events. He rose at six every morning and read the morning papers cover to cover. He also had phones that were directly connected to the exchanges in Paris, London, Chicago, and New York, and talked often to the traders on the floor.

He was also a person who went broke several times from taking tips. Often, the tips will be given to you with the best of intentions. They may come from friends, even relatives, so they will sound very appealing. They may even emanate from insiders in a company (officers and directors) that have perhaps created a new technology or a revolutionary product and you may be told that the company is about to announce the breakthrough. Such a tip, also is dangerous because it may really come true, and the stock pops upward. Then the trader is remorseful that he did not act on the tip . . . so he may take the next tip he gets. It was Livermore's life experience that these tips rarely paid off, and in the long term, they often cost him a lot of money. His final rule—*take no tips—not ever* . . . period.

CHAPTER 8

General Livermore Issues

Every stock is like a human being: It has a personality—a distinctive personality—aggressive, reserved, hyper, high-strung, volatile, boring, direct, logical, predictable, unpredictable. Livermore often studied stocks as you would study people, after a while their reactions to certain circumstance become more predictable.

Livermore was not the first to observe this. There are traders who have made a lot of money in the stock market by just analyzing the personality of a stock and following that personality, reacting to it by buying and selling it according to its personality traits. But beware—not often, but sometimes, personalities change.

Livermore firmly believed that as long as a stock was acting properly—progressing, with normal reactions such as consolidations, corrections, and proceeding in the direction of the trend—there was nothing to fear, no reason for a speculator to concern himself. And the fact that a stock is selling in new high territory should only encourage the speculator.

On the other hand, a speculator must never become complacent or relaxed to the point that he misses the clues that the stock has topped out and is creating a Pivotal Point that will set it off in a new direction, perhaps a reversal in trend. The lesson: Be ever-vigilant, alert, for the danger signs.

The essentials to stock market success are *knowledge and patience*. Few people succeed in the market, mostly because they have no patience. They have a strong desire to get rich quickly. They buy mostly when a stock is going up and is near the top. They are not willing to buy when the

127

stock goes down and wait until it forms a pivotal point and begins to re-cover—if it does recover.

In the long run, patience counts more than any other single element except knowledge. The two really go hand in hand. Those who want to succeed through their investments should learn that simple truth. You must also investigate before you buy; then you are sure your posi-tion is sound.

Never become discouraged by the fact that your securities are moving slowly. Good securities in time appreciate sufficiently to make it well worthwhile to have patience.

The only time to buy is when you know a stock will go up. These situ-ations come along only rarely—the trader must wait, be patient; sooner or later the right situation will come along.

In trading to beat the game, a big part is the right timing. Livermore's quest was never ending: to refine and develop the Pivotal Point approach, his approach to trading new highs, finding the industry leaders and the best industry group. These stock-trading theories were all developed after much experience and effort. But it was the mental challenge that was al-ways his passion and challenge.

But like all traders, he also enjoyed what the money could do.

WHEN DOES A STOCK ACT RIGHT?

Markets never stand still. They are very dull at times, but they are not rest-ing at one price. They are either moving up or down, if only a fraction.

When a stock gets into a definite trend, it works automatically and consistently along certain lines throughout the progress of its move.

At the beginning of the move, you will notice a very large volume of sales with gradually advancing prices for a few days. Then what Liv-ermore termed a Normal Reaction will occur. On that reaction, the sales volume will be much less than on the previous days of its advance. That little reaction is only normal. Never be afraid of the normal move-ment. But be very fearful of abnormal movements, like a major change in personality.

In a day or two, activity will start again, and the volume will increase. If it is a real movement, in a short space of time the natural, normal reac-tion will have been recovered, and the stock will be selling in new high territory. That movement should continue strong for a few days with only minor daily reactions.

Sooner or later, it will reach a point where it is due for another normal reaction. When it occurs, it should be along the same lines as the first reaction, because that is the natural way any stock will act when it is in a definite trend.

At the first part of a movement of this kind, the distance above the previous high point to the next high point is not very great. But as time goes on, you will notice that it is making much faster headway on the upside.

Take a stock that starts at 50. On the first leg of the movement, it might gradually sell up to 54. A day or two of normal reaction might carry it back to 52. Three days later, it is on its way again. In that time it might go up to 59 or 60 before the normal reaction would occur.

But instead of reacting, say, only a point or a point and one-half, a natural reaction from that level could easily be 3 points. When it resumes its advance again in a few days, you will notice that the volume of sales at that time is not nearly as large as it was at the beginning of the move—the stock is becoming harder to buy.

That being the case, the next points in the movement should be much more rapid than before. The stock could easily go from the previous high of 60 to 68 or 70 without encountering a natural reaction.

When that normal reaction does occur, it could be more severe. It could easily react down to 65 and still have only a normal decline. But assuming that the reaction was five points or thereabouts, it should not be many days before the advance would be resumed, and the stock should be selling at a brand new high price. And that is where the Livermore time element comes into play. Don't let the stock go stale on you. After attaining a good profit, you must have patience, but don't let patience create a frame of mind that ignores the danger signals. Always be on the alert. Don't be lulled into complacency.

A danger signal: The stock starts up again, and it has a rise of six or seven points in one day, followed the next day by perhaps eight to ten points—with great activity—but during the last hour of the day all of a sudden it has an abnormal break of seven or eight points. The next morning, it extends its reaction another point or so, and then once more starts to advance, closing very strong. But the following day, for some reason, it does not carry through.

This is an immediate danger signal.

All during the progress of the move, it had nothing but natural and normal reactions. Then all of a sudden an abnormal reaction occurs—and by abnormal I mean a reaction in one day of six or more points from an extreme price made in that same day —something it has not had before. When something happens abnormally in the stock's normal pattern, it is flashing you a danger signal that must not be ignored.

You have had patience to stay with the stock all during its natural progress. Now have the courage and good sense to honor the danger signal and step aside.

This is not to say that these danger signals are always correct because, as stated before, no rules applying to stock fluctuations are 100 percent right. But if you pay attention to them consistently, in the long run you will profit immensely.

A speculator of great genius once told Livermore: "When I see a danger signal handed to me, I don't argue with it. I get out! A few days later, if everything looks all right, I can always go back in again. Thereby I have saved myself a lot of worry and money. I figure it out this way. If I were walking along a railroad track and saw an express train coming at me sixty miles an hour, I would be a damned fool not to get off the track and let the train go by. After it had passed, I could always get back on the track again, if I desired."

Every judicious speculator must always be on the alert for danger signals.

Curiously, the trouble with most speculators is that something inside of them keeps them from mustering enough courage to close out their commitment when they should. They hesitate, and during that period of hesitation they watch the market go many points against them. Then they say: "On the next rally I'll get out!" When the next rally comes, as it will eventually, they forget what they intended to do, because in their opinion the market is acting fine again. However, that rally was only a temporary swing that soon plays out, and then the market starts to go down in earnest. And they are still in it—due to their hesitation. If they had been using a guide, it would have told them what to do; not only saving them a lot of money but eliminating their worries.

As mentioned, emotion is the greatest enemy of the average investor or speculator. Why shouldn't a stock rally after it starts down from a big advance? Of course it will rally from some level, if the stock is basically all right financially. But why hope it is going to rally at just the time you want it to rally? Chances are it won't, and if it does, the vacillating type of speculator may not take advantage of it.

Banish wishful thinking. A trader cannot be successful by speculating every day or every week. There are only a few times a year, possibly four or five, when you should allow yourself to make any real commitment at all. In the interims, you are letting the market shape itself for the next big movement. If you have timed the movement correctly, your first commitment will show you a profit at the start. From then on, all that is required of you is to be alert, watching for the appearance of the danger signal to tell you to step aside and convert paper profits into real money.

Remember this: When you are doing nothing, those speculators who feel they must trade day in and day out are laying the foundation for your next venture. You will reap benefits from their mistakes.

Speculation is far too exciting for most people; most people who speculate hound the brokerage offices or receive frequent telephone calls, and after the business day they talk stock market with friends at all gatherings. Trading is always on their minds. They are so engrossed with the minor ups and downs that they miss the big movements.

Almost invariably, the vast majority have commitments on the wrong side of the market when the broad trend swings get under way. The speculator who insists on trying to profit from daily minor movements may miss the next important change when it occurs.

TIME—THE FOURTH DIMENSION IN TRADING

Livermore heard a story that had a great effect on him about a remarkably successful speculator who lived in the California mountains and received quotations three days old. Two or three times a year, he would call on his San Francisco broker and begin writing out orders to buy or sell, depending upon his market position. A friend of Livermore's, who spent time in the broker's office, became curious and made inquiries. His astonishment mounted when he learned of the man's extreme detachment from market facilities, his rare visits, and, on occasion, his tremendous volume of trades.

Finally, he was introduced to the trader from the mountains, and in the course of conversation inquired of this man from the mountains how he could keep track of the stock market at such an isolated distance.

"Well," the man replied, "I make speculation a business. I would be a failure if I were in the confusion of things and let myself be distracted by minor changes. I like to be away where I can think. You see, I keep a record of what has happened, after it has happened, and it gives me a rather clear picture of what markets are doing.

"Real movements do not end the day they start. It takes time to complete the end of a genuine movement. By being up in the mountains I am in a position to give these movements all the time they need. But a day comes when I get some prices out of the paper and put them down in my records. I notice the prices I record are not conforming to the same pattern of movements that has been apparent for some time.

"Right then I make up my mind. I go to town and get busy!"

Consistently, the man from the mountains, over a long period of time, drew funds in large quantities from the stock market. He was something of an inspiration to Livermore. After hearing this story, Livermore went to work harder than ever trying to blend the element of time with all the other data he had compiled. By constant effort, he was able to bring his

records into a coordination that aided him to a surprising degree in anticipating coming movements.

The dimension of time (not timing) was the last element that fascinated Jesse Livermore. He was studying it in detail at the time of his death
He believed that *in the stock market, time is not money—time is time—
and money is money.*

THE MARKET OPERATES IN FUTURE TIME

Every successful trader must understand that the market does not operate
in present time; it operates in future time. The current market of 2004 bottomed out in October of 2002, forming a clear Reversal Pivotal Point. (See
Figure 8.1.) This went basically unnoticed by most traders, mutual funds,
and media pundits. Livermore would have loved it!

Behind all major movements in the stock market are irresistible forces
at work. This is all the successful speculator needs to know. Just be aware

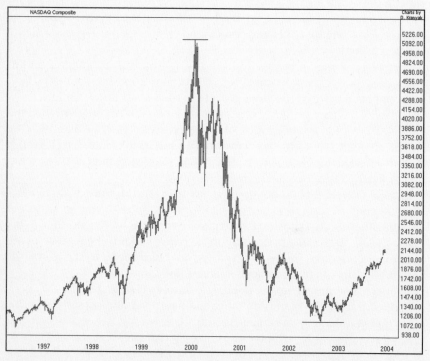

Figure 8.1 The Nasdaq shows two Reversal Pivotal Points 1997–2004.

of the actual stock movements, and act upon that knowledge. It is too difficult to match up world events or current events or economic events, with
stock market movements. This is true because the stock market always
moves ahead of world events. The stock market is not operating in the present or reflecting the present; it is operating on what is yet to be, the future.
The market often moves contrary to apparent common sense and world
events, as if it had a mind of its own, designed to fool most people, most of
the time. Eventually, the truth of why it moved as it did will emerge.

It is foolish to try and anticipate the movement of the market based
on current economic news and current events, such as the balance of pay-
ments, Consumer Price Index, and the unemployment figures, even the ru-
mor of war, because these are usually already factored into the market.
Livermore did not ignore these facts or remain ignorant of them—he was-
n't. But these were not facts he could ever use to *predict* the market. After
the market moved, it would be rationalized in endless post mortems by
the financial pundits, and later when the dust had settled, the real economic, political, and world events would eventually be brought into focus
by historians as to the actual reasons why the market acted as it had. But
by that time it was too late to make any money.

Trying to figure out the why of a market move can often cause great
emotional strife. The simple fact is, the market always precedes economic
news; it does not usually react to economic news for any sustained period.
It must be understood by the astute trader that the market lives and operates in future time. For example, a good earning statement is issued by a
company and the stock proceeds to fall in price—why? Because the market had already factored in those earnings.

TIME AS A TRADING DIMENSION

Later in Livermore's trading history, he decided that he would not hold
stocks for long that did not move in the direction he had anticipated. If he
had followed his rules and waited for what he considered to be the perfect
time to buy the stock, and if it did not move as he believed it should move
within a few days or what he considered a reasonable time, he would then
sell out the position. He would wait days, weeks, months, for the stock to
position itself at the spot he thought most opportune, in other words the
perfect moment to make his purchase—when every factor was in his favor. If the stock did not do as expected, he would often sell out his entire
position, even if the stock did not decline.

Why? Because the successful trader must try and keep his money cir-
culating as a merchant must keep his inventory moving, so he can keep

the inventory fresh. The one thing he had learned in his many years of playing the stock market was that there are always opportunities in the market, so to remain with your cash in a stand-by position meant that your money, your inventory, was inactive now, but this could yield huge benefits in the future, when it was finally committed to that special situation. Just as it is true that many people will sell their good stocks and keep their losers it is true that they will also keep the stocks that are flat, not doing anything or going anywhere.

Please be aware that this does not mean a stock will not have a normal correction or a normal consolidation in an upward trend. What we are talking about here is a stock that is just wallowing in a trading channel, making no progress in either direction. It must be determined whether the stock is being accumulated or is being distributed. If it is not clear, then it is sometimes best to exit the stock than to take a chance that it is being distributed and will eventually move against you and go down and cost you money. Give the stock a little time to show itself in these situations, but waste no time in closing out an inconclusive stock and moving on to another trading situation.

Livermore often sold a stock that had even moved a point or two in his favor, but he simply did not like the weak or limp manner in which it was acting. It did not matter to him—even if he had a small profit or a small loss—the major fact remained the stock did not do what he had analyzed and believed that it would do. So the conclusion was obvious and always simple to him—his judgment had been wrong and therefore he must exit the trade.

One thing he knew for sure was that his judgment had been wrong in the past and that it would be wrong again in the future. The danger was in not recognizing his mistakes and getting out in time. The old adage is correct—pride often does come before a fall.

The worse kinds of stocks are what he called Listless Drifters. These are stocks that do not move in the desired manner and simply tie up a stock market trader's capital as they hang out there drifting in no man's land. Whenever Livermore was forced to depend on hope, he always felt exposed to danger. When he simply took his loss, he knew what it was, and he know what he would have to make back to get into profit. Also, if he stayed with the losing or listless position, it had a negative psychological effect and always bothered him as he moved ahead with future trades.

Livermore discovered that he could not afford to trade in anything but live stocks, stocks that are leading the pack, stocks that have inherent energy. This energy, or momentum, always meant trading on both sides of the market—the upside and the downside, long or short.

He observed many, many people who purchased stocks and put them away in safe deposit boxes or safes, feeling that their investments were safe. These were the thoughts that people had for the stocks of steel, radio, aircraft, oil, railroads, and hundreds of other safe-as-money-in-the-bank securities that all eventually went sour in his day. This was never true in Livermore's view: One can never assume that a stock can be bought and put away for the future.

It was essential for Livermore to keep his capital in circulation. Remember, when a merchant has part of his capital frozen out of circulation he must then make all his profit on the capital that is left. This hampers and hinders him because that unfrozen capital must often work twice as hard to make up for the dead, frozen capital, which yields little or nothing.

It must also be understood by the trader that in the Livermore Trading System, money sitting in cash was not deemed to be capital out of circulation. It was considered reserve capital waiting to be used at the propitious moment when it could bring in huge returns, as it often did for Livermore.

But above and beyond this reasoning are what he called *lost opportunities*. Because their capital is frozen, these stock traders miss many golden opportunities to trade the winners, the stocks that would have bought them profits and success—profits that were unavailable because their capital was tied up in stagnant, unprofitable situations.

Hope is the villain here, and it has ruined millions of traders over the course of time—take your losses right away; after all, they are real whether you sell the stocks or not.

As a result of this thinking about the dimension of time, Livermore initiated a new technique into his trading system near the end of his life, a technique that is still revolutionary in its thinking, even in today's stock market.

Livermore used two stops when he entered a trade, a *price stop* and a *time stop*. These were combined with his thinking that he would not stay with any trade more than a few points if it moved against him, and he would not stay with a stock position for more than a few days if the stock did not perform as he expected.

This became the lifeblood of his trading system because it was how he kept his capital in working circulation. It may sound contradictory, but it isn't; there are times when he was out of the market completely with all his working capital in cash, waiting and waiting for the market to choose a trend and for the perfect trading scenario to re-present itself to him.

"Often money that is sitting can later be moved into the right situation at the right time and make you a vast fortune. Patience, Patience, Patience is the key to success, not speed; time is a cunning speculator's best friend, if he uses it correctly.

"Remember the clever speculator is always patient and has a reserve of cash."

—Jesse Livermore

The concept of time will be even more challenging in the coming decades as worldwide stock markets become digitalized and trade electronically (with no human help). The Toronto Stock Exchange and the German Dax have already converted to electronic markets that operate with no hands-on help from human beings. This will eventually result in worldwide 24-hour-a-day trading. One of the unpredictable aspects, however, is that a person could go to sleep and awake in the morning with deep losses or healthy profits.

Please note, the concept of global trading—or trading following the rising sun, beginning in Japan and ending in the United States—is a reality that is not far away from common usage. It is actually possible to do this now, and it is being done currently by a handful of ambitious traders, who often go without sleep.

Livermore used a week as his rough time frame in deciding whether he would hold a stock that he had purchased and that did not act as he predicted. In other words, he would give a stock five trading days to move after he had acquired it.

As already stated, his reasoning was simple: "I have waited until what I believe is the perfect moment to pull the trigger on a stock, and go ahead and buy a stock or sell it short. If the stock does not perform, then something is wrong with my judgment, because I thought everything was ready when I pulled the trigger . . . it is obvious if the stock does not do as I anticipated, then I have not analyzed the situation correctly . . . therefore I must cancel out the trade and not wait for the stock to act right. As in all similar cases, the solution will be revealed to me at a later date."

What was novel and important here is that: *The stock did not have to move against Livermore* for him to sell it. The stock could remain flat or near the price he purchased it. It could simply lie languishing. The point to Livermore was that whatever it is doing, it is not doing what he had expected it to do, so his safest bet was to get out of the trade and move on or perhaps go back into the situation after the move had been confirmed.

This is a far more difficult concept to execute than may appear to the average trader. Emotionally, it becomes a struggle, since the trader may not have lost any money in the trade. It may be recalled that Livermore also said a trader needs a reason to buy a stock and a reason to sell. This technique provides the reason: The stock did not do what it was supposed to when it was bought! This was a good enough reason for Livermore to close out the trade. This is an essential factor in the Livermore Stock Trading System.

One of the main challenges for a trader is to identify the current leaders and to spot the new leaders who are waiting to take over from the current ones. During major shifts and changes in market direction, it is of paramount importance to observe the leaders that are being driven out and identify the new stocks that will assume the leadership in the future.

It is usually best to go with the strongest stock in the strongest group—do not look for the cheapest or the laggard stock that has not yet had his turn to move in the group—always go for the strongest most dominant stock in the group. In the long run, this will pay off.

Livermore's theories and methods came from his never-ending study of the market. He believed a trader is always a student of the market, never a master. Like a ship's captain who studies the oceans, the tides, the moon, his fellow shipmates, the construction of his ship, and the stars for navigation, he knows he can never be in complete control, for a variety of reasons. He knows the biggest reason is that he cannot control the weather, the weather is in the hands of God and nature.

Livermore knew that the market is comprised of human beings, and human beings are mostly driven by emotion not logic. He knew that people were often unpredictable and not like the stars in the heavens with a reliable pattern or the tides that rise and fall as predicted. With humans, nothing in their behavior is certain except uncertainty. A good stock trader must, in the end, be a student of human behavior, but he can improve his odds by placing the highest probabilities on his side. In Livermore's case, he made several fortunes by doing this correctly. In every case, his theories were based on actual trading experience. His thinking was way ahead of its time, and even today much of his thinking revolutionary and inspiring. His vision of the dimension of *time* and how it applies to trading stock is one of those factors.

The Time Stop

And please add to your trading arsenal what Livermore stated before: "I always have two stops in mind when I enter a trade: I have a *price stop* and I have a *time stop*. I will not stay with any trade more than a few points if it moves against me and I will not stay with a stock position for more than a few days or perhaps up to a week, if the stock does not perform as I expect it to perform. And there is still much more for traders to do on the subject of time in the future, as technology and the human knowledge base continues to expand."

HISTORY REPEATING ITSELF

Livermore believed that the game of speculation is the most uniformly fascinating game in the world. But it is not a game for the stupid, the mentally lazy, or the person of inferior emotional balance, or for the get-rich-quick adventurer. They will die poor.

Over a long period of years, he rarely attended a dinner party including strangers when someone did not sit down beside him and inquire after the usual pleasantries:

"How can I make some money in the market?"

In his younger days, he went to considerable pains to explain all the difficulties faced by the trader who simply wishes to take quick and easy money out of the market; or through courteous evasiveness, he would work his way out of the snare.

In later years, his answer became a blunt "I don't know."

It was difficult for him to exercise patience with such people. In the first place, the inquiry is not a compliment to a man like Jesse Livermore who has made a scientific study of investment and trading.

It would be similar for the layman to ask an attorney or a surgeon: "How can I make some quick money in law or surgery?"

It is simply hard work, constant study, discipline, and unyielding perseverance that leads the way to success in the stock market, as it does in any profession. But before we go further, let me warn you that the fruits of your success will be in direct ratio to the honesty and sincerity of your own effort in keeping your own records, doing your own thinking, and reaching your own conclusions.

You cannot read a book on how to keep fit and leave the physical exercises to someone else. Nor can you delegate to another the task of keeping your records. You must understand and follow faithfully Livermore's stock trading system, and understand and combine all the aspects of Timing, Money Management, and Emotional Control, as set forth in these pages. Livermore could only lead the way, and he would be a happy man if through his guidance, a trader would be able to take more money out of the stock market than he put in.

This information is for that portion of the public that at times may be speculatively inclined. Some points and ideas are presented here that come directly from Livermore's many years as an investor and speculator. Anyone who is inclined to speculate should look at speculation as a business and treat it as such, and not regard it as a pure gamble, as so many people are apt to do.

If the premise that speculation is a business in itself, those engaging in that business should determine to learn and understand it to the best of their ability, using all the data available. In the forty years that he devoted to making speculation a successful business venture, Livermore was still discovering new rules to apply to that business. The stock market is a journey with no end.

On many occasions, Livermore went to bed wondering why he had not been able to foresee a certain imminent move, and awakened in the early hours of the ensuing morning with a new idea formulated, actually impatient for the morning to arrive in order to start checking over his records of past movements to determine whether the new idea had merit. In most cases, it was far from being 100 percent right, but what good there was in it was stored in his subconscious mind. Perhaps, later, another idea would take form, and he would immediately set to work checking it over.

In time, these various ideas began to crystallize, and he was able to develop a concrete method of keeping records in such a form that he could use them as a guide.

His conclusion was that nothing new ever occurs in the business of trading or investing in securities or commodities. There are times when one should speculate, and just as surely there are times when one should not speculate.

There is a very true adage that Livermore loved: "You can beat a horse race, but you can't beat the races."

So it is with market operations. There are times when money can be made investing and speculating in stocks, but money cannot consistently be made by trading every day or every week during the year. Only the foolhardy will try it.

To invest or trade successfully, one must form an opinion as to what the next move of importance will be in a given stock. Speculation is nothing more than anticipating coming movements. In order to anticipate correctly, one must have a definite basis for that anticipation, rules to follow, but one has to be careful because people are often not predictable—they are full of emotion—and the market is made up of people. The good speculators always wait and have patience, waiting for the market to confirm their judgment.

For instance, analyze in your own mind the effect that a certain piece of news may have in relation to the market. Try to anticipate the psychological effect of this particular item on the market. If you believe it likely to have a definite bullish or bearish effect on the market, don't back your judgment—*wait until the action of the market itself confirms your opinion*. The effect on the market may not be as pronounced as you are inclined to believe it should be. Do not anticipate and move without market confirmation—being a little late in your trade is your insurance that you are right or wrong.

To illustrate further: After the market has been in a definite trend for a given period, a bullish or bearish piece of news may not have the slightest effect on the market, or it may have a temporary effect. The market itself at the time may be in an overbought or oversold condition, in which case the effect of that particular news would certainly be ignored. At such times, the recording value of past performances under similar conditions becomes of inestimable value to the investor or speculator.

At such times you must entirely ignore personal opinion and apply strict attention to the action of the market itself.

Markets are never wrong—opinions often are.

The latter are of no value to the investor or speculator unless the market acts in accordance with his ideas.

No one man, or group of men, can make or break a market today. One may form an opinion regarding a certain stock and believe that it is going to have a pronounced move, either up or down, and eventually be correct in one's opinion, but one will lose money by presuming or acting too soon. Believing his opinion to be right, the trader acts immediately, only to find that after he has made his commitment the stock goes the other way. The market becomes narrow; he becomes tired and gets out. Perhaps a few days later it begins to look all right, and in he goes again, but no sooner has he re-entered than the stock turns against him once more. Once more, he begins to doubt his opinion and sells out. Finally, the move starts up. Having been too hasty and having made two unprofitable commitments, he loses courage. It is also likely that he has made other commitments and is not in a position to assume more. Thus, by the time the real move in the stock he jumped into prematurely is on, he is out of it.

The point to emphasize here is that after forming an opinion with respect to a certain stock, do not be too anxious to get into it. Wait and watch the action of that stock for confirmation to buy. Have a fundamental basis to be guided by.

Experience proved to Livermore that the real money made in trading was in *commitments to a stock or commodity that show a profit right from the start.*

Livermore's trading operations were mostly driven by Pivotal Point action. As already explained, he always attempted to make his first trade at the right psychological time, that is, at a time when the force of the movement was so strong that it simply had to carry through. It simply had to and did go. But there were many times in his career when, like many other speculators, he did not have the patience to await the sure thing, because he wanted to have an interest in the market at all times.

With all his experience, why did he allow himself to do so? The answer is that Livermore was human and subject to human weakness. Like all speculators, he permitted impatience to outmaneuver good judgment.

Profits always take care of themselves but losses never do.

The speculator has to insure himself against considerable losses by taking the first small loss. In so doing, he keeps his account in order, so that at some future time, when he has a constructive idea, he will be in a position to go into another deal, taking on the same amount of stock as he had when he was wrong.

The speculator has to be his own insurance broker, and the only way he can continue in business is to guard his capital account and never permit himself to lose enough to jeopardize his operations at some future date when his market judgment is correct.

There are definitely certain times when a reversal in trend rally gets under way, and at this time an astute trader can devise a specific method (rules) to use as a guide, which will permit him to judge correctly when to make his initial commitment. Successful speculation is not a mere guess. To be consistently successful, an investor or speculator must have rules to guide him. Certain guides that one trader, such as myself, utilizes may be of no value to anyone else, so the trader may want to create his own combination of methods to trade the market. Independent thinking was Livermore's hallmark, and there are many ways to successfully trade the stock market.

No guide to trading can be 100 percent right. So, if a stock does not act as you anticipated, you must immediately determine that the time is not yet ripe and close out the commitment.

Perhaps a few days later your guide indicates you should get in again, so back you can go, and perhaps this time it is 100 percent correct. Livermore was convinced that anyone who will take the time and trouble to study the market carefully should in time be able to develop a guide that will aid him in future operations or investments.

Livermore said, "A great many traders keep charts or records of averages. They chase them around, up and down, and there is no question that these charts of averages do point out a definite trend at times. Personally, charts have never appealed to me. I think they are altogether too confusing. Nevertheless, I am just as much of a fanatic in keeping records as other people are in maintaining charts. They may be right, and I may be wrong.

"My preference for records is due to the fact that my recording method gives me a clear picture of what is happening. But it was not until I began to take into consideration the element of time and timing that my records really became useful in helping me to anticipate coming movements of importance. I believe that by keeping proper records and taking the time element into consideration, one can with a fair degree of accuracy forecast coming movements of importance. But it takes patience to do so.

"Familiarize yourself with a stock, or different groups of stocks, and if you figure the timing element correctly in conjunction with your records, sooner or later you will be able to determine when a major move is due. If you read your records correctly, you can pick the leading stock in any group.

"Traders must keep their own records. Don't let anyone else do it for you. You will be surprised how many new ideas you will formulate in so doing; ideas which no one else could give you, because they are your discovery, your secret, and you should keep them your secret."

CHAPTER 9

Livermore Quotes— Trading Truths

J esse Livermore is perhaps the most quoted trader in stock market history.

The extensive quote section that follows has been organized by categories that align with the structure of this book. They should be helpful to all traders.

ANTICIPATION

By constant effort I was able to bring my records into a co-ordination that aided me to a surprising degree in anticipating coming movements.

To invest or speculate successfully, one must form an opinion as to what the next move of importance will be in a given stock.

In order to anticipate correctly, one must have a definite basis for that anticipation.

It was not until I began to take into consideration the time element that my records really became useful in helping me to anticipate coming movements of importance.

Just as soon as you familiarize yourself with the actions of the past, you will be able to anticipate and act correctly and profitably upon forthcoming movements .

I do know a basis for anticipating future movements and if anyone will study these records, keeping them themselves, they cannot fail to profit by it in their operations.

This sense of knowing when you are wrong even before the market tells you becomes, in time, rather highly developed. It is a subconscious tip-off. It is a signal from within that is based on knowledge of past market performances. I am always suspicious of this inner mind tip-off and usually prefer to apply the cold scientific formula. But the fact remains that on many occasions I have benefited to a high degree by giving attention to a feeling of great uneasiness.

This curious sidelight on trading is interesting because the feeling of danger ahead seems to be pronounced only among those sensitive to market action, those whose thoughts have followed a scientific pattern in seeking to determine price movements.

From these records one can visualize a map useful in determining the approach of important price movements.

BUYING

Do not buy a stock because it has had a big decline from its previous high.

It may surprise many to know that in my method of trading, when I see by my records that an upward trend is in progress, I become a buyer as soon as a stock makes *a new high on its movement, after having had a normal reaction.*

I never buy on reactions or go short on rallies.

Each succeeding purchase must be at a "higher price" than the previous one.

When your chosen stock reaches the point you had previously decided it should reach if the move is going to start in earnest, that is the time to make your first commitment.

So it is plain to see why your friend, the industrialist on the inside, can easily tell you when to buy. But he cannot and will not tell you when to sell. That would be equivalent almost to treason to his associates.

GROUP ACTION/LEADERS

That break-out to a new high movement (the stock will be selling in new high territory) should continue strong for a few days with only minor daily reactions. Sooner or later it will reach a point where it is due for another normal reaction. When it (the normal reaction) occurs, it should be on the same lines as the first reaction, because that is the natural way any stock will act when it is in a definite trend.

Familiarize yourself with a stock, or different groups of stocks, and if you figure the timing element correctly in conjunction with your records, sooner or later you will be able to determine when a major move is due.

What I wish to impress upon you is the fact that when you clearly see a move coming in a particular group, act upon it.

Have patience and wait. In time you will get the same tip-off in other groups that you received in the first group.

If you cannot make money out of the leading active issues, you are not going to make money out of the stock market as a whole.

In the course of time new leaders will come to the front; some of the old leaders will be dropped. It will always be that way as long as there is a stock market.

Remember the leaders of today may not be the leaders two years from now.

It is when you set down prices in your record book and observe the patterns that the prices begin to talk to you.

I would explain that I do not take the action of a single stock as an indication that the trend has been positively changed for that group.

LOSSES

Traders often hesitate as a stock declines, and during that period of hesitation they watch the market go many points against them.

Profits always take care of themselves, but losses never do.

The speculator has to insure himself against considerable losses by taking the first small loss.

It would be simple to run down the list of hundreds of stocks, which, in my time, have been considered gilt-edge investments, and which today are worth little or nothing.

Thus, great investments tumble, and with them the fortunes of so-called conservative investors in the continuous distribution of wealth.

I believe it is a safe statement that the money lost by speculation alone is small compared with the gigantic sums lost by so-called investors who have let their investments ride.

A good trader will, by acting promptly, hold his losses to a minimum and await a more favorable opportunity to reenter the market.

It is foolhardy to make a second trade, if your first trade shows you a loss.

"Never average losses." Let that thought be written indelibly upon your mind.

But it is not necessary to lose your money, once you have acquired it, if you will hold fast to sound principles.

Every time I lost patience and failed to await the Pivotal Points and fiddled around for some easy profits in the meantime, I would lose money. My loss was due wholly to lack of patience in awaiting the proper time to back up a pre-conceived opinion and plan.

The market will tell the speculator when he is wrong, because he is losing money.

When a trader first realizes he is wrong, that is the time to clear out, take his losses, study the record to determine the cause of the error, and await the next big opportunity.

MARKET ACTION

Markets never stand still.

They are very dull at times, but they are not resting at one price. They are either moving up or down a fraction.

At the beginning of the move you will notice a very large volume of sales with gradually advancing prices for a few days.

Never be afraid of the normal movement. But be very fearful of abnormal movements, it is similar to a major change in personality.

Short-term traders are often so engrossed with the minor ups and downs that they miss the big movements.

Almost invariably the vast majority have commitments on the wrong side when the broad trend swings are well under way.

The speculator who insists on trying to profit from daily minor movements will never be in a position to take advantage of the next important change marketwise when it occurs.

Real movements do not end the day they start. It takes time to complete the end of a genuine movement.

Don't back your judgment *until the action of the market itself confirms your opinion.* . . .

Markets are never wrong —opinions often are.

You will notice I always tried to make my first trade at the psychological time, that is, at a time where the force of the movement was so strong that it simply had to carry through.

Your trade may grow into a very large profit, and as long as the *action of the market does not give you any cause to worry, have the courage of your convictions and stay with it.*

I do not use the words bullish or bearish in defining trends of the market because I think so many people when they hear the words bullish or bearish spoken of marketwise immediately think that is the course the market is going to take for a very long time.

Well-defined trends of that kind do not occur very often—only once in about four or five years— but during that time there are also many well-defined trends which last for a comparatively short time.

I consequently use the words *"Upward Trend"* and *"Downward Trend,"* because they fully express what is going on at that specific time.

The Livermore Stock Trading Method, my method, of recording prices in conjunction with the time element is the result of over thirty years of study of principles that would serve me in forming a basic guide for the next important market movement.

Frequently I had observed that when a stock sold at 50, 100, 200 and even 300, a fast and straight movement almost invariably occurred after such points were passed.

Bear in mind when using Pivotal Points in anticipating market movements, that if the stock does not perform as it should, after crossing the Pivotal Point, this is a danger signal that must be heeded.

I learned the main thing was to watch the follow-through as it crossed through the Pivotal Point.

I knew that in due time, when the upward trend had reached its Pivotal Point, I would be given a danger signal in ample time.

Whenever the market does not act right or in the way it should, that is reason enough for you to change your opinion and change it immediately.

MONEY MANAGEMENT

The speculator has to insure himself against considerable losses by taking the first small loss.

The speculator has to be his own insurance broker, and the only way he can continue in business is to guard his capital account and never permit himself to lose enough to jeopardize his operations at some future date when his market judgment is correct.

Therefore the investor must guard his capital account just as the successful speculator does in his speculative ventures.

When you are handling surplus income do not delegate the task to anyone.

So, at the risk of repetition and preaching, let me urge you to avoid averaging down. I know but one sure tip I got from a broker. It is your "Margin Call—When the margin call reaches you, close your account—never meet a margin call." You are on the wrong side of the market.

A person engaged in the business of speculation should risk only a limited amount of capital on any one venture.

Cash to the speculator is as merchandise on the shelves of the merchant.

A speculator should make it a rule each time he closes out a successful deal to take one-half of his profits and lock this sum up in a safe deposit box.

The only money that is ever taken out of Wall Street by speculators is the money they draw out of their accounts after closing a successful deal.

The only time the average speculator can draw money from his brokerage account is when he has no position open or when he has an excessive equity.

Money in a broker's account or in a bank account is not the same as if you feel it in your own fingers once in a while.

When a speculator is fortunate enough to double his original capital he should at once draw out one half of his profit to be set-aside for reserve.

In consideration of these general trading principles it should be said that too many speculators buy or sell impulsively, acquiring their entire line at almost one price. That is wrong and dangerous.

Having made that commitment, decide definitely the amount of money you are willing to risk should your calculations be wrong.

PROFITS

After attaining a goodly profit, you must have patience, but don't let patience create a frame of mind that ignores the danger signals.

But if you pay attention to them (danger signals) consistently, in the long run you will profit immensely.

If you have timed the movement correctly, your first commitment will show you a profit at the start.

From then on, all that is required of you is to be alert, watching for the appearance of the danger signal to tell you to step aside and convert paper profits into real money.

The speculator who insists on trying to profit from daily minor movements will seldom be in a position to take advantage of the next important change marketwise when it occurs.

Experience has proved to me that the real money made in speculating has been in commitments in a stock or commodity showing a profit right from the start.

As long as a stock is acting right, and the market is right, do not be in a hurry to take a profit.

You know you are right, because if you were not, you would have no profit at all.

It may grow into a very large profit, and as long as the "action of the market "does not give you any cause to worry, have the courage of your convictions and stay with it.

Incidentally, every time I lost patience and failed to await the Pivotal Points and fiddled around for some easy profits in the meantime, I would lose money.

You will discover that profits made in this way are immensely more gratifying than any which could possibly come from the tips or guidance of someone else.

The fact that your trades "DO" show you a profit is proof you are right.

I was often altogether too anxious to convert a paper profit into actual cash, when I should have been patient and had the courage to play the deal out to the end.

SHORTING

Many have lost their capital funds by selling a stock short after a long upward movement, when it "seemed too high."

I never buy on reactions or go short on rallies.

I found it was an easy matter for me to turn around and get out of a position, when vitality was lacking after a stock crossed the Pivotal Point and there were many occasions when I reversed my position and went over to the short-side.

That same rule should be applied in selling short. Never make an additional sale unless it is at a lower price than the previous sale.

This illustrates the value of having a short interest in speculative markets because the short interests become willing buyers when they cover their shorts, and those-willing buyers, the short sellers, act as a much-needed stabilizer in times of panic.

STOCKS

Stocks, like individuals, have a character and a personality. Some are high-strung, nervous, and jumpy—others are forthright, direct, logical.

A skillful trader comes to know and respect individual securities. Their action is predictable under varying sets of conditions.

When a stock gets into a definite trend, it works automatically and consistently along certain lines throughout the progress of its move.

Then what I term a "Normal Reaction" will occur. On that reaction the sales volume will be much less than on the previous days of its advance.

To invest or speculate successfully, one must form an opinion as to what the next move of importance will be in a given stock.

Familiarize yourself with a stock, or different groups of stocks, and if you figure the timing element correctly in conjunction with your records, sooner or later you will be able to determine when a major move is due.

When a stock starts sliding downward, no one can tell how far it will go. Nor can anyone guess the ultimate top on a stock in a broad upward movement.

TRADING/SPECULATION

I do not say that danger signals are always correct, no rules applying to stock fluctuations are 100 percent right.

When I see a danger signal handed to me, I don't argue with it. I get out! A few days later, if everything looks all right, I can always go back in again.

Every judicious speculator is on the alert for danger signals.

Curiously, the trouble with most speculators is that something inside of them keeps them from mustering enough courage to close out their bad commitment when they should.

Again let me say, the human side of every person is the greatest enemy of the average investor or speculator.

What I am trying to make clear to that part of the public which desires to regard speculation as a serious business, and I wish deliberately to reiterate it, is that wishful thinking must be banished.

The speculator who insists on trying to profit from daily minor movements will never be in a position to take advantage of the next important change marketwise when it occurs.

I make speculation a business. I would be a failure if I were in the confusion of things and let myself be distracted by minor changes. I like to be away where I can think.

The game of speculation is the most uniformly fascinating game in the world. But it is not a game for the stupid, the mentally lazy, the man of inferior emotional balance, or for the get-rich-quick adventurer. They will die poor.

I have come to the conviction, however, that larger numbers of people interested in stock-market investment and speculation would be willing to work and study to attain sensible results, if they had a guide or signpost pointing the right direction.

Out of it all emerges my theory of "time element in trading, which I regard as the most important factor in successful speculation.

But before we go further, let me warn you that the fruits of your success will be in direct ratio to the honesty and sincerity of your own effort in keeping your own records, doing your own thinking, and reaching your own conclusions.

You cannot wisely read a book on "How to keep fit" and leave the physical exercises to another.

Anyone who is inclined to speculate should look at speculation as a "business" and treat it as such and not regard it as a pure gamble as so many people are apt to do.

If I am correct in the premise that speculation is a business in itself, those engaging in that business should determine to learn and understand it to the best of their ability with informative data available.

My theory and practical application have proved to my satisfaction that nothing new ever occurs in the business of speculating or investing in securities or commodities.

There are times when one should speculate, and just as surely there are times when one should not speculate.

There are times when money can be made investing and speculating in stocks, but money cannot consistently be made trading every day or every week during the year.

To invest or speculate successfully, one must form an opinion as to what the next move of importance will be in a given stock.

No one man, or group of men, can make or break a market today.

Experience has proved to me that the real money made in speculating has been in commitments in a stock or commodity showing a profit right from the start.

It is a human trait to be hopeful and equally so to be fearful, but when you inject hope and fear into the business of speculation, you are faced with a very formidable hazard, because you are apt to get the two confused and in reverse positions.

The speculator has to insure himself against considerable losses by taking the first small loss.

The speculator has to be his own insurance broker, and the only way he can continue in business is to guard his capital account and never permit himself to lose enough to jeopardize his operations at some future date when his market judgment is correct.

Successful speculation is not a mere guess.

To be consistently successful, an investor or speculator must have rules to guide him. Certain guides that I utilize may be of no value to anyone else.

One of the primary "DON'T'S" is—one should never permit speculative ventures to run into investments. Don't become an "Involuntary Investor."

There is always the temptation in the stock market, after a period of success, to become careless or excessively ambitious.

One major mistake of all speculators is the urge to enrich themselves in too short a time.

Often for people who enter the speculative field 25 percent is nothing. They are looking for 100 percent. And their calculations are faulty; they fail to make speculation a business and run it on business principles. The lesson here again is that speculation itself is a business and should be so viewed by all.

Do not permit yourself to be influenced by excitement, flattery or temptation.

The speculator wants to trade and the broker not only is willing, but too often encourages over-trading.

The uninformed speculator regards the broker as his friend and is soon over-trading.

Never make any trade unless you know you can do so with financial safety.

Whenever I have had the patience to wait for the market to arrive at what I call a "Pivotal Point" before I started to trade; I have always made money in my operations.

I found it was an easy matter for me to turn around and get out of a position, when vitality was lacking after a stock crossed the Pivotal Point and there were many occasions when I reversed my position and went over to the short-side.

Nevertheless, there are other ways by which one can determine Pivotal Points.

You will derive from successful trades based on your own judgment a singular pleasure and satisfaction.

If you make your own discovery, trade your own way, exercise patience, and watch for the danger signals, you will develop a proper trend of thinking.

Few people ever make money by trading on the occasional tips or recommendations of others. Many beg for information and then don't know how to use it.

Nevertheless, in making speculation a business, one automatically keeps an eye on all markets for the big opportunities.

It would not surprise me if the persons who in the future follow my methods of keeping these records get even more out of them than I have.

Someone else, however, may develop from this basic method new ideas which, when applied, will enhance the value of my basic method for their purpose.

In consideration of these general trading principles it should be said that too many speculators buy or sell impulsively, acquiring their entire line at almost one price. That is wrong and dangerous.

It was too depressing, a mood not conducive to the clear thinking that is required at all times in the field of speculation . . . to allow myself to become angry and disgusted with the cotton market just because I had used bad judgment was not consistent with good speculative procedure.

I have long since learned, as all should learn, not to make excuses when wrong. Just admit it and try to profit by it. We all know when we are wrong.

The market will tell the speculator when he is wrong, because he is losing money.

Bear in mind that of the millions who speculate in all markets only a few devote their entire time to speculation.

Beware of inside information . . . All inside information!

It cannot be said too often that in speculation and investment, success comes only to those who work for it.

No one is going to hand you a lot of easy money.

And if there was any easy money lying around, no one would be forcing it into your pocket.

I hold the firm belief that the future successful careful investor will only operate at the psychological time and will eventually realize a much larger percentage out of every minor or major movement than the purely speculative-minded operator ever did.

The intent is to catch the major moves, to indicate the beginning and the end of movements of importance.

VOLUME

In a day or two activity will start again, and the volume will increase. If it is a real movement, in a short space of time the natural, normal reaction will have been recovered, and the stock will be selling in new high territory.

WHAT TO TRADE

I mean, do not have an interest in too many stocks at one time. It is much easier to watch a few than many, ten at the most—five is better. Definitely it is not safe to try to keep account of too many stocks at one time. You will become entangled and confused.

Confine your studies of movements to the prominent stocks of the day.

Try to analyze comparatively few groups. You will find it is much easier to obtain a true picture that way than if you tried to dissect the whole market.

Commodities frequently offer attractive Pivotal Points.

TIMING WHEN TO TRADE

And that is where the "time element" comes in. Don't let the stock go stale on you.

You have had patience to stay with the stock all during its natural progress. Now have the courage and good sense to honor the danger signal and step aside.

A trader cannot be successful by speculating every day or every week; there are only a few times a year, possibly four or five, when you should allow yourself to make any commitment at all.

If you have timed the movement correctly, your first commitment will show you a profit at the start.

Remember this: When you are doing nothing, those speculators who feel they must trade day in and day out, are laying the foundation for your next venture.

Such weaknesses can be corrected by keeping and studying records of stock price movements and how they occur, and by taking the time element carefully into account.

Out of it all emerges my theory of "the time element" in trading, which I regard as the most important factor in successful speculation.

You cannot delegate to another the task of keeping your records, if you are to follow faithfully my formula for combining the time element and prices as set forth in subsequent pages.

One may form an opinion regarding a certain stock and believe that it is going to have a pronounced move, either up or down, and eventually be correct in his opinion, but will lose money by presuming or acting on his opinion too soon.

The point I would here emphasize is that after forming an opinion with respect to a certain stock—do not be too anxious to get into it. First, wait and watch the action of that stock or stocks marketwise.

Have patience and wait until the stock becomes active, until it makes a new high.

There have been many times when I, like many other speculators, have not had the patience to await the sure thing. I wanted to have an interest at all times.

I am human and subject to human weakness. Like all speculators, I permitted impatience to out-maneuver good judgment.

But it was not until I began to take into consideration the time element that my records really became useful in helping me to anticipate coming movements of importance.

Familiarize yourself with a stock, or different groups of stocks, and if you figure the timing element correctly in conjunction with your records, sooner or later you will be able to determine when a major move is due.

Try to forget a stock's past high range and study it on the basis of the formula that combines timing and price.

It may surprise many to know that in my method of trading, when I see by my records that an upward trend is in progress, I become a buyer as soon as a stock makes a "new high on its movement, after having had a normal reaction."

It has always been my experience that I never benefited much from a move if I did not get in at somewhere near the beginning of that move.

Just as markets in time will give you a positive tip when to get in—if you have patience to wait—they will just as surely give you a tip-off when to get out.

Rome was not built in a day, and no real movement of importance ends in one day or in one week. It takes time for it to run its logical course.

It is significant that a large part of a market movement occurs in the last forty-eight hours of a play, and that is the most important time to be in it.

The Livermore Method, my method, of recording prices in conjunction with the time element is the result of over thirty years of study of principles that would serve me in forming a basic guide for the next important market movement.

From the time I started to merge the time element with price movements, my records began to talk to me!

When a speculator can determine the Pivotal Point of a stock and interpret the action at that point, he may make a commitment with the positive assurance of being right from the start.

This again illustrates the rewards that go to the person who has the patience to wait for and take advantage of the Pivotal Points.

By keeping stock price records and taking into consideration the time element, you will be able to find many Pivotal Points on which to make a commitment for a fast movement.

But by being consistent and never failing to re-enter the market again whenever your Pivotal Point is reached, you cannot help but be in when the real move does occur.

But careful timing is essential . . . impatience costly.

My losses were often due wholly to lack of patience in awaiting the proper time to back up a preconceived opinion and plan.

I was often altogether too anxious to convert a paper profit into actual cash, when I should have been patient and had the courage to play the deal out to the end.

I knew when the upward trend had reached its Pivotal Point, I would be given a danger signal in ample time.

Certainly success with this plan depends upon courage to act, and act promptly, when your records tell you to do so. There is no place for vacillation.

If you are going to wait upon someone else for explanations or reasons or reassurances, the time for action will have escaped.

There is folly in trying to find "a good logical reason" why you should buy or sell a given stock. If you wait until you have the reason given you, you will have missed the opportunity of having acted at the proper time!

CHAPTER 10

Summary of Livermore Trading Rules

*D*on't concern yourself with why things are happening only observe what is happening. The reasons why will eventually be revealed to you—by then it will be too late to make money! The move will be over.

Learn from your mistakes, analyze them. The trick is not to repeat your mistakes, which meant to Livermore you had to first understand them—find out what went wrong with the trade and don't repeat the same mistake again.

Place as many factors in your favor as possible. Livermore was successful when *all* the factors were in his favor, and he concluded that the more factors he could think of the more successful he would be.

No trader can or should play the market all the time. There will be many times when you should be out of the market, sitting in cash, waiting patiently for the perfect trade.

Determine the direction of the overall market. Livermore referred to this as the Line of Least Resistance. He did not use the terms "bull" or "bear" for a very specific reason: he felt these terms caused a mind set to form: the market is in a Bullish Trend or the market is in a Bearish Trend. This in turn caused the trader to have a mindset that would anticipate the direction of a trade or the direction of the market—a deadly and dangerous thing to do.

Don't try and anticipate what the market will do next—simply go with the evidence of what the market is telling you—presenting to you. Experience has proved to me that the real money made in speculating has been in commitments in a stock or commodity showing a profit right from the start.

Profits always take care of themselves but losses never do. The speculator should insure himself against considerable losses by taking the first small loss. In so doing, he keeps his account in order so that at some future time, when he has a constructive idea, he will be in a position to go into another deal, taking on the same amount of stock as he had when he was wrong.

As long as a stock is acting right, and the market is right, do not be in a hurry to take a profit. You know you are right, because if you were not, you would have no profit at all. Let it ride and ride along with it. It may grow into a very large profit, and as long as the action of the market does not give you any cause to worry, have the courage of your convictions and stay with it.

Do not have an interest in too many stocks at one time. Remember that it is dangerous to start spreading out all over the market. It is much easier to watch a few than many. I made that mistake years ago and it cost me money.

A successful speculator remains a constant student of three things:

1. *Market timing*—When to enter and when to exit a market trade–when to hold 'em when to fold 'em, as Livermore's friend and Palm Beach Casino owner Ed Bradley used to say.

2. *Money management*—Don't lose money—don't lose your stake, your line. A speculator without cash is like a store owner with no inventory. Cash is a speculator's inventory, his lifeline, his best friend—without it you're out of business. *Don't lose your line!*

3. *Emotional control*—Before you can successfully play the market you must have a clear, concise strategy and stick to it. Every speculator must design an intelligent battle plan, customized to suit his emotional makeup, before speculating in the stock market. The biggest thing a speculator has to control are his emotions. Remember, the stock market is not driven by reason, logic, or pure economics, but by human nature which never changes. How can it change? It's our nature.

You can't tell if your judgment is right until you put your money on the line. If you don't put your money on the table you can never test your judgment, because you can never test your emotions. And I believe it is emotion, not reason that dictates the direction of the stock market, just like most important things in life: love, marriage, children, war, sex, crime, passion, religion. It is rarely reason that drives people.

This is not to say things like sales, profits, world conditions, politics, and technology do not play a part in the ultimate price of a stock. These factors eventually come to bear, and the price of the stock market and the individual stocks may reflect them, but it is always emotion that carries the extremes.

The market moves in cycles. I believe in cycles, in life cycles and market cycles. They are often extreme, hardly ever balanced. Cycles come like a series of ocean waves, bringing the high tide when things are good and, as conditions recede, the low tide appears. These cycles come unexpectedly, unpredictably, and they have to be weathered with temperance, poise, and patience-good or bad. The stock market is a study in cycles, when it changes direction it remains in that new trend until the momentum weakens—a body in motion tends to stay in motion—remember, don't buck the trend—don't fight the tape. The skillful speculator knows that money can be made no matter what the market conditions, if a speculator is willing to play both sides of the market, as I was.

SHORT LIST OF LIVERMORE MARKET RULES

I long ago realized that the stock market is never obvious. It is designed to fool most of the people, most of the time. My rules are often based on thinking against the grain, against human nature:

- Cut your losses quickly;
- Be sure to confirm your judgment before you take your full position;
- Let your profits ride if there is no good reason to close out the position;
- The action is with the leading stocks, these can change with every new market;
- Keep the number of stocks you follow limited in order to focus;
- New all-time highs are possible signals of valid break-outs;
- Cheap stocks often appear to be bargains after a large drop. They often continue to fall, or have little potential to rise in price. Leave them alone!
- Use Pivotal Points to identify trend changes and confirmations in trends;
- Don't fight the tape!

Play both sides of the market. In a free market system, *Prices fluctuate!* They never go up all the time, and they never go down all the time. This is good for the alert speculator, since either side of the market can be played.

The market goes up a third of the time, sideways a third of the time, and down a third of the time. If a trader only takes long positions he is out of the play two-thirds of the time. Going short of stocks can be very profitable for the astute trader.

Cut Losses Quickly.   Never sustain a loss of more than 10 percent of your invested capital. This Livermore learned in the bucket shops where he worked with 10 percent margin and was automatically sold out if the loss exceeded the 10 percent limit. This is also a money management rule.

Wait until all the factors are in your favor before making a trade— follow the Top Down Trading rules.   The big money is made by the sitting—the waitin'—not the thinking. Once a position is taken, the next difficult task is to be patient and wait for the move to play out. The temptation is strong to take fast profits or cover your trade solely out of fear of losing the profit on a correction. This error has cost millions of speculators millions of dollars. Be sure you have good clear reasons to enter a trade, and be sure you have good clear reasons to exit your position. It is the big swing that makes the big money for you.

Play the market only when all factors are in your favor.   No person can play the market all the time and win. There are times when you should be completely out of the market.

Cover your losses quickly, without hesitation.The only thing to do when a person is wrong is to be right, by ceasing to be wrong. Don't waste time, when a stock moves below a mental-stop, sell it immediately.

Study the stocks like you would study people. After a while their reactions to certain circumstances become predictable, and useful, in timing the stock's movement.   Stocks often act like human beings, expressing different personalities: aggressive, reserved, hyper-high-strung, direct, logical, predictable, unpredictable.

Stocks are never too high to begin buying or too low to begin selling short.

Failure to take the opportunity to get out of large illiquid positions when the opportunity presents itself can cost.

Failure to take advantage of a serendipitous act of good luck in the stock market is often a mistake.

Don't anticipate! Wait for market confirmation!   In a market moving sideways in a narrow channel where stock prices are essentially stagnant, there is a great danger in trying to predict or anticipate *when*, and in what *direction* the market will move. You must wait until the market or the stock breaks out of this sideways channel in either direction. Never argue with the tape. Follow the line of least resistance. Follow the evidence.

The answer always lies in what the tape says, not trying to figure out the why.   Do not spend a lot of time trying to figure out what moves the price of a particular stock. Rather, examine the tape. Behind all major movements in the stock market there is an irresistible force, which will most likely be revealed later. That is all the successful speculator needs to know.

The stock market goes up, down and sideways. You can make money on the up side or the down side-you can buy long or sell short. It should not matter to you what side of the market you are on. You must be impersonal. When the market goes sideways and you are confused, take a vacation.

Beware of the one-day reversal. When the high of the day is higher than the high of the previous day, but the close of the day is below the close or the low of the previous day and the volume of the current day is higher than the volume of the previous day, beware!

If the stock you traded is going in the opposite direction than you expected, sell it quickly. It means your judgment was wrong—cut your losses quickly.

Study the action of a stock that has made a severe break in price, a precipitous drop. If the stock does not rebound quickly it will most likely fall away further—there is an inherent weakness in this stock, the reason will be revealed at a later time.

The market is operating in future time. It has usually already factored in current events.

A change in trend, if caught, yields the most rewards. It is the inception of a basic movement, the Pivotal Point, a change in trend, which indicates whether to buy or sell.

Pivotal Points are an essential timing device, a trigger that reveals when to enter, and when to exit the market. There are two kinds of Pivotal Points: The Reversal Pivotal Point and the Continuation Pivotal Point. The Reversal Pivotal Point is defined as the *perfect psychological time at the beginning of a major market move, a change in basic trend.* It does not matter if it is at the bottom or top of a long-term trending move. It marks a definite change in direction. The Continuation Pivotal Point confirms the move is underway—it is a natural consolidation before the next move upward. Be alert—major Pivotal Points can often be accompanied by a heavy increase in volume.

At the end of a bull market, watch for wild capitalizations, good stocks selling at 30, 40, 50, 60 times their annual earnings. These will be the same stocks that had normally traded at 8 to 12 times earnings.

Beware of wild speculative stocks that take off for no real reasons, except that they are trendy, in-favor stocks.

New highs are very important for timing. A new all-time high can mean that the stock has broken through the overhead supply of stock and the line of least resistance will be strongly upward. The majority of people, when they see that a stock has made a new high, sell it immediately, then look for a cheaper stock.

Top Down Trading—follow the trend—check the main market.   The speculator must know the overall trend of the market before making a trade—*the line of least resistance.* Know if this line of *least resistance* is upward or downward. This applies to both the overall market and individual stocks. The basic thing you need to know before making a trade is which way the overall market is headed, up, down, or sideways. You have to decide this first before making a trade. If the overall trend of the market is not in your favor, you are playing at an extreme disadvantage, remember, go with the flow, bend with the trend, do not sail into a gale, and most of all . . . don't argue with the tape!

Group action is a key to timing.   Stocks do not move alone when they move. If U.S. Steel climbs in price, then sooner or later Bethlehem, Republic, and Crucible will follow. The premise is simple: If the basic reasons are sound why U.S. Steel's business should come into favor in the stock market, then the rest of the steel group should also follow for those same reasons.

Trade the leading stocks in the leading groups—as the leaders go so goes the entire market.   Buy the strongest market leader in an industry group.

Watch the market leaders, the stocks that have led the charge upwards in a bull market. When these stocks falter and fail to make new highs, it is often a signal that the market has turned. Confine your studies of stock market movements to the prominent issues of the day, the leaders. If you cannot make money out of the leading active issues, you are not going to make money out of the stock market. That is where the action is and where the money is to be made. It also keeps your universe of stocks limited, focused, and more easily controlled.

Before you buy a stock, you should have a clear target where to sell if the stock moves against you, a firm stop.   And you must obey your rules!

Buy small positions, probe first, to test your judgment before you commit to a large position.   A successful market trader must only bet on the course of highest probabilities. Do not establish your full position all at one time—use probes to confirm your judgment and timing and to find the line of *least resistance.* The *probe approach* is also a major factor in Money Management.

The trader must react quickly to the unexpected, which is never predictable.   If it is a windfall, grab it. If it is bad news, hit the road, and don't look back or hesitate—sell out the position.

Beware after a long trend up when volume gets heavy, and stocks churn.   This is a clue, a red-alert warning that the end of the move is near. This is also a possible indication of stocks going from strong hands to weak hands, from the professional to the public, from accumulation to distribution. The public often views this heavy volume as the mark of a vibrant, healthy market going through a normal correction, not a top or a bottom.

Follow money management rules:

Establish stops! The speculator should have a clear target where to sell if the stock moves against you. This is essential on the first buys—trailing stops can also be used as the stock moves, although I always did these with trailing mental stops. And you must obey your rules! Never sustain a loss of more than 10 percent of your invested capital. Losses can be twice as expensive to make up. I learned this in the bucket shops working with 10 percent margin. You were automatically sold out by the bucket shops if the loss exceeded the 10 percent limit.

Never sustain a loss of more than 10 percent of invested capital. The 10 percent loss rule is an important rule for managing money. As noted, this is also a key timing rule. If you lose 50 percent, you must gain 100 percent to break even.

Livermore 10 Percent Loss Table

Starting Position	*Amount Lost*	*Remainder*	*% Loss*	*% to Recover Loss*
$1000	$ 80	$920	8.0	8.7
	100	900	10.0	11.1
	200	800	20.0	25.0
	300	700	30.0	42.8
	400	600	40.0	66.6
	500	500	50.0	100.0

Never meet a margin call and never average down in your buying.

Turn paper profits into "real money" periodically. Take a percent of your winnings and put them in a safe place, like the bank or bonds, or an annuity. Cash was—is—and always will be—king.

Always have cash in reserve. Cash is the ammunition in your gun. My biggest mistake was not in following this rule more often.

Examine and understand the dimension of time:

Don't be in a hurry. The successful investor is not invested in the market all the time—there are many times when you should be completely in cash. If you are unsure of the direction of the market, then stay out and wait for a confirmation of the next move.

Use probes to establish your full position. After an initial probe, do not make a second move until the first probe shows you a profit. Do not establish your full position all at once, wait until your first trades, your early probes, have shown you a profit, then go ahead and fill out your full position. To be precise: First establish 20 percent of your planned position on the first purchase, 20 percent on the second, 20 percent on the third. Wait for a confirmation of your judgment—then make your final purchase of 40 percent. Consider each of these purchases, or probes, a crucial factor in establishing the overall position. If at any time the stock goes against you, then wait or close out all your positions, never sustaining more than a 10 percent loss of invested capital.

Sell the losers, let the winners ride, provided all the factors are positive.

SUMMARY OF FIVE KEY MONEY MANAGEMENT RULES

- Protect your capital—use probing system to buy
- Observe the 10 percent bucket shop rule
- Keep cash in reserve
- Stick with the winners—let your profits ride—cut your losses
- Take 50 percent of your big winnings off the table

EMOTIONAL CONTROL

Emotional control is the most essential factor in playing the market. Never lose control of your emotions when the market moves against you. And never become elated with your successes to such a degree that you think the market is an easy way to make money. Never fight the tape—the tape is the truth . . . seek harmony with the tape.

Don't anticipate! Wait until the market gives you the clues, the signals, the hints, before you move. Move only after you have confirmation. Anticipation is the killer. It is the brother to greed and hope. Don't make decisions based on anticipation. The market always gives you time. If you wait for the clues, there will be plenty of time to execute your moves.

All stocks are like human beings, with different personalities: aggressive, reserved, hyper, high-strung, direct, dull, old fashioned, futuristic, logical, illogical. Study the stocks as you would study people; after a while, their reactions to certain circumstance become predicable. Some traders limit their trading to stocks in specific price ranges.

Do not spend a lot of time trying to figure out why the price of a particular stock moves. Rather, examine the facts themselves. The answer lies in *what* the tape says, not trying to figure out *why*, and most importantly—*never argue with the tape.*

A stock trader can be convinced to move away from his own convictions by listening to the advice of other traders, persuaded that his judgment may be faulty. Listening to others may cause indecision and bad judgment. This indecision may cause a loss of confidence, which may well mean a loss of money.

Tips come from many sources—from a relative, a loved one, a pal who has just made a serious investment himself and wants to pass on his expected good fortune. They also come from hucksters and criminals. Remember: *All tips are dangerous—take no tips!*

Remove hope from your trading lexicon. Hoping a stock will do something is the true form of gambling. If you do not have good solid reasons to hold stock positions, then move on to another more logical trade. Wishing a stock up, or down, has caused the downfall of many stock market speculators. Hope walks along hand in hand with greed.

Always be aware of your emotions—don't get too confident over your wins or too despondent over your losses. You must achieve poise, a balance in your actions.

Nothing ever changes in the market. The only thing that changes are the players, and the new players have no financial memory of the previous major cycles, like the Crash of 1907, or the Crash of 1929, because they have not experienced them. It may be new to the speculator—but it's not new to the market.

Always have a method of speculating, a plan of attack. And always stick to your plan. Do not constantly change your plan. Find a method that works emotionally and intellectually for you, and stick to that method—stick to your own customized rules.

The speculator is not an investor. His object is not to secure a steady return on his money over a long period of time. The speculator must profit by either a rise or fall in the price of whatever he has decided to speculate in.

Play a lone hand. Make your decisions about your own money by yourself. Be secretive and silent in your stock trading. Do not disclose your winners or your losers.

The successful investor is not invested in the market all the time— there are many times when you should be completely in cash. If you are unsure of the direction of the market, wait.

It takes four strong *mental characteristics* to be a superior market trader:

- *Observation*: the ability to observe the facts without prejudice;
- *Memory*: the ability to remember key events correctly, objectively;
- *Mathematics*: an easy facility with numbers, at home with digits;
- *Experience*: to retain and learn from your experiences.

Livermore believed that subliminal messages, apparent impulses, were nothing more than the subconscious mind talking to him; calling up his experiences, his years of trading. On occasion, Livermore would let his inner-mind lead him, even if he didn't know exactly why at the time. Livermore believed Aristotle, who said, *"We are the sum total of our experience."*

Emotions must be understood and harnessed before successful speculation is possible:

Greed is a human emotion defined by Webster's dictionary as the *excessive desire for acquiring or possessing, a desire for more than one needs or deserves.* We do not know the origin of greed, all we know is that it exists in every person.

Fear lays ready to appear in a single heartbeat, and when it does, it twists and distorts reason. Reasonable people act unreasonably when they are afraid. And they get afraid every time they start to lose money. Their judgment becomes impaired.

Hope lives hand in hand with greed when it comes to the stock market. Once a trade is made, hope springs alive. It is human nature to be hopeful, to be positive, to hope for the best. Hope is important to the survival of the human race. But hope, like its stock market cousins, ignorance, greed, and fear, distorts reason. Hope clouds facts, and the stock market only deals in facts. Like the spinning of a roulette wheel, the little black ball tells the outcome—not greed, fear, or hope. The result is objective and final with no appeal . . . like nature.

Ignorance.   The market must be studied and learned, not in a casual way, but in a deep knowledgable way. Like no other entity, the stock market, with its allure of easy money and fast action, induces people into the foolish mishandling of their money. The reverse of ignorance is knowledge, and knowledge is power.

The stock market is never obvious.   It is designed to fool most of the people, most of the time. Livermore's rules are often based on thinking against the grain.

You should not be in the market all the time.   There are times you should be out of the market, for emotional as well as economic reasons.

When the tape doesn't agree with your decision to buy or sell, wait until it does.   Never try to rationalize your position with what the tape is saying.

Do not give or receive stock tips, just remember: In a bull market stocks go up-in a bear market they go down.   That is all anyone needs to know, or for you to tell them.

Do not break your rules. A stock speculator sometimes makes mistakes, and knows that he is making them, but proceeds anyway, only to berate himself later for breaking his own rules.

Never become an involuntary investor by holding a declining stock.

Never buy a stock on reactions, and never short a stock on rallies.

Do not use the words bullish *or* bearish. These words fix a firm market direction in the mind for an extended period of time. Instead, use Upward Trend and Downward Trend when asked the direction you think the market is headed. Simply say: "The line of least resistance is either upward, or downward at this time, as I did."

Speculation is a business, and like any other business it takes hard work and diligence to succeed.

CONCLUSION

"There is nothing new on Wall Street or in stock speculation. What has happened in the past will happen again, and again, and again. This is because human nature does not change, and it is human emotion that always gets in the way of human intelligence.

Of this I am sure."

—Jesse Livermore

CHAPTER 11

Livermore Secret Market Key

The Livermore Market Key section in this book is exactly as it was written in the 1940 version, originally published by Duell, Sloan and Pearce (New York). All explanatory charts have also been added in their original condition. This section of the book contains reprints of his actual worksheets; complete with Livermore's own day-to-day comments on his system as it applied to actual market action in specific stocks. The only change has been to replace color with black-and-white designations. What were originally blue numbers now appear black; the original red numbers are black and boxed; and what were black numbers are black and circled. Red double underscores now appear black and dashed, while the black double underscores haven't changed.

The prudent stock market student, after reading and studying this section, will observe that some of the numbers used by Livermore as examples are difficult to follow. We have attempted to understand these various examples, even so far as going to the second edition, which was published in 1966 by Investor's Press, Inc. (Palisades Park, N.J.). Our objective was to see if there were any problems with the actual worksheets that we may not have noticed in the original 1940 published version.

There were no discrepancies—this is exactly as Livermore presented his Market Key Theory.

The Livermore Market Key

Many years of my life had been devoted to speculation before it dawned upon me that nothing new was happening in the stock market, that price movements were simply being repeated, that while there was variation in different stocks the general price pattern was the same.

The urge fell upon me, as I have said, to keep price records that might be a guide to price movements. This I undertook with some zest. Then I began striving to find a point to start from in helping me to anticipate future movements. That was no easy task.

Now I can look back on those initial efforts and understand why they were not immediately fruitful. Having then a purely speculative mind, I was trying to devise a policy for trading in and out of the market all the time, catching the small intermediate moves. This was wrong, and in time I clearly recognized the fact.

I continued keeping my records, confident that they had a genuine value which only awaited my discovery. At length the secret unfolded. The records told me plainly that they would do nothing for me in the way of intermediate movements. But if I would but use my eyes, I would see the formation of patterns that would foretell major movements.

Right then I determined to eliminate all the minor movements.

By continued close study of the many records I had kept the realization struck me that the *time element* was vital in forming a correct opinion as to the approach of the really important movements. With renewed vigor I concentrated on that feature. What I wanted to discover was a method of recognizing what constituted the minor swings. I realized a market in a definite trend still had numerous intermediate oscillations. They had been confusing. They were no longer to be my concern.

I wanted to find out what constituted the beginning of a Natural Reaction or a Natural Rally. So I began checking the distances of price movements. First I based my calculations on one point. That was no good. Then two points, and so on, until finally I arrived at a point that represented what I thought should constitute the beginning of a Natural Reaction or Natural Rally.

To simplify the picture I had printed a special sheet of paper, ruled in distinctive columns, and so arranged as to give me what I term my Map for Anticipating Future Movements. For each stock I use six columns. Prices are recorded in the columns as they occur. Each column has its heading.

First column is headed Secondary Rally.
Second is headed Natural Rally.

Third is headed Upward Trend.
Fourth is headed Downward Trend.
Fifth is headed Natural Reaction.
Sixth is headed Secondary Reaction.

When figures are recorded in the Upward Trend column they are entered in black ink. In the next two columns to the left I insert the figures in pencil. When figures are recorded in the Downward Trend column they are entered in red ink, and in the next two columns to the right, the entries are also made in pencil.

Thus when recording the prices either in the Upward Trend column or in the Downward Trend column I am impressed with the actual trend at the time. Those figures in distinctive ink talk to me. The red ink [now black and boxed] or the black ink [still black but circled], used persistently, tells a story that is unmistakable.

When the pencil remains in use I realize I am simply noting the natural oscillations. (In the reproduction of my records later on, bear in mind that the prices entered in light blue ink [now black] are those for which I use a pencil on my sheets.)

I decided a stock selling around $30.00 or higher would have to rally or react from an extreme point to the extent of approximately six points before I could recognize that a Natural Rally or Natural Reaction was in the making. This rally or reaction does not indicate that the trend of the market has changed its course. It simply indicates that the market is experiencing a natural movement. The trend is exactly the same as it was before the rally or reaction occurred.

I would here explain that I do not take the action of a single stock as an indication that the trend has been positively changed for that group. Instead I take the combined action of two stocks in any group before I recognize the trend has definitely changed, hence the Key Price. By combining the prices and movements in these two stocks I arrive at what I call my Key Price. I find that an individual stock sometimes has a movement big enough to put it in my Upward Trend column or my Downward Trend column. But there is danger of being caught in a false movement by depending upon only one stock. The movement of the two stocks combined gives reasonable assurance. Thus, a positive change of the trend must be confirmed by the action of the Key Price.

Let me illustrate this Key Price method. Strictly adhering to the six-point movement to be used as a basis, you will note in my subsequent records that at times I record a price in U.S. Steel if it only has had a move, let us say, of $5\frac{1}{8}$ points because you will find a corresponding

(Continued)

movement in Bethlehem Steel, say, of 7 points. Taken together the price movements of the two stocks constitute the Key Price. This Key Price, then, totals twelve points or better, the proper distance required.

When a recording point has been reached, that is, a move of six points average by each of the two stocks, I continue to set down in that same column the extreme price made any day, whenever it is higher than the last price recorded in the Upward Trend column or is lower than the last price recorded in the Downward Trend column. This goes on until a reverse movement starts. This later movement in the other direction will, of course, be based on the same six-point average, or twelve points for the Key Price.

You will notice that from then on I never deviate from those points. I make no exceptions. Nor do I make excuses, if the results are not exactly as I anticipated. Remember, these prices I set forth in my records are not my prices. These points have been determined by actual prices registered in the day's trading.

It would be presumptuous for me to say I had arrived at the exact point from which my record of prices should start. It would also be misleading and insincere. I can only say that after years of checking and observation I feel I have arrived somewhere near a point that can be used as a basis for keeping records. From these records one can visualize a map useful in determining the approach of important price movements.

Someone has said that success rides upon the hour of decision. Certainly success with this plan depends upon courage to act and act promptly when your records tell you to do so. There is no place for vacillation. You must train your mind along those lines. If you are going to wait upon someone else for explanations or reasons or reassurances, the time for action will have escaped. To give an illustration: After the rapid advance stocks had following the declaration of war in Europe, a Natural Reaction occurred in the whole market. Then all the stocks in the four prominent groups recovered their reaction and all sold at new high prices—with the exception of the stocks in the Steel group. Anyone keeping records according to my method would have had their attention drawn very forcefully to the action of the Steel stocks. Now there must have been a very good reason why the Steel stocks refused to continue their advance along with the other groups. There was a good reason! But at the time I did not know it, and I doubt very much that anyone could have given a valid explanation for it. However, anyone who had been recording prices would have realized by the action of the Steel stocks that the upward movement in the Steel group had ended. It was not until the middle of January 1940, four months later, that the public was given the facts and the action of the Steel stocks was explained. An announcement was made that during that time the English Government had disposed of over 100,000 shares of U.S. Steel, and in addition Canada had sold 20,000 shares. When that announcement was made the price of U.S. Steel was 26 points lower than its high price attained in September 1939 and Bethlehem Steel was 29 points lower, whereas the prices of the other three prominent groups were off only 2 to 12¼ points from the high prices that were made at the same time the Steels made their highs. This incident proves the folly of trying to find out a good reason why you should buy or sell a given stock. If you wait until you have the reason given you, you will have missed the opportunity of having acted at the proper time! The only reason an investor or speculator should ever want to have pointed out to him is the action of the market itself. Whenever the market does not act right or in the way it should—that is reason enough for you to change your opinion and change it immediately. Remember: there is always a reason for a stock acting the way it does. But also remember: the chances are that you will not become acquainted with that reason until some time in the future, when it is too late to act on it profitably.

I repeat that the formula does not provide points whereby you can make additional trades, with assurance, on intermediate fluctuations which occur during a major move. The intent is to catch the major moves, to indicate the beginning and the end of movements of importance. And for such purpose you will find the formula of singular value if faithfully pursued. It should, perhaps, also be repeated that this formula is designed for active stocks selling above an approximate price of 30. While the same basic principles are of course operative in anticipating the market action of all stocks, certain adjustments in the formula must be made in considering the very low-priced issues.

There is nothing complicated about it. The various phases will be absorbed quickly and with easy understanding by those who are interested.

In the next chapter is given the exact reproduction of my records, with full explanation of the figures which I have entered.

Explanatory Rules

(1) Record prices in Upward Trend Column in black ink.

(2) Record prices in Downward Trend column in red ink.

(3) Record prices in the other four columns in pencil.

(4) (a) Draw red [black and dashed] lines under your last recorded price in the Upward Trend column the first day you start to record figures in the Natural Reaction column. You begin to do this on the first reaction of

(Continued)

approximately six points from the last price recorded in the Upward Trend column.

(b) Draw red [black and dashed] lines under your last recorded price in the Natural Reaction column the first day you start to record figures in the Natural Rally column or in the Upward Trend column. You begin to do this on the first rally of approximately six points from the last price recorded in the Natural Reaction column. You now have two Pivotal Points to watch, and depending on how prices are recorded when the market returns to around one of those points, you will then be able to form an opinion as to whether the positive trend is going to be resumed in earnest—or whether the movement has ended.

(c) Draw black lines under your last recorded price in the Downward Trend column the first day you start to record figures in the Natural Rally column. You begin to do this on the first rally of approximately six points from the last price recorded in the Downward Trend column.

(d) Draw black lines under your last recorded price in the Natural Rally column the first day you start to record figures in the Natural Reaction column or in the Downward Trend column. You begin to do this on the first reaction of approximately six points from the last price recorded in the Natural Rally column.

(5) (a) When recording in the Natural Rally column and a price is reached that is three or more points above the last price recorded in the Natural Rally column (with black lines underneath), then that price should be entered in black ink [and circled] in the Upward Trend column.

(b) When recording in the Natural Reaction column and a price is reached that is three or more points below the last price recorded in the Natural Reaction column (with red [black and dashed] lines underneath), then that price should be entered in red ink [black and boxed] in the Downward Trend column.

(6) (a) When a reaction occurs to an extent of approximately six points, after you have been recording prices in the Upward Trend column, you then start to record those prices in the Natural Reaction column, and continue to do so every day thereafter that the stock sells at a price which is lower than the last recorded price in the Natural Reaction column.

(b) When a reaction occurs to an extent of approximately six points, after you have been recording prices in the Natural Rally column, you then start to record those prices in the Natural Reaction column, and continue to do so every day thereafter that the stock sells at a price which is lower than the last recorded price in the Natural Reaction column. In case a price is made which is lower than the last recorded price in the Downward

Trend column, you would then record that price in the Downward Trend column.

(c) When a rally occurs to an extent of approximately six points, after you have been recording prices in the Downward Trend column, you then start to record those prices in the Natural Rally column, and continue to do so every day thereafter that the stock sells at a price which is higher than the last recorded price in the Natural Rally column.

(d) When a rally occurs to an extent of approximately six points, after you have been recording prices in the Natural Reaction column, you then start to record those prices in the Natural Rally column, and continue to do so every day thereafter that the stock sells at a price which is higher than the last recorded price in the Natural Rally column. In case a price is made which is higher than the last recorded price in the Upward Trend column, you would then record that price in the Upward Trend column.

(e) When you start to record figures in the Natural Reaction column and a price is reached that is lower than the last recorded figure in the Downward Trend column then that price should be entered in red ink [black and boxed] in the Downward Trend column.

(f) The same rule applies when you are recording figures in the Natural Rally column and a price is reached that is higher than the last price recorded in the Upward Trend column—then you would cease recording in the Natural Rally column and record that price in black ink [and circled] in the Upward Trend column.

(g) In case you had been recording in the Natural Reaction column and a rally should occur of approximately six points from the last recorded figure in the Natural Reaction column—but that price did not exceed the last price recorded in the Natural Rally column—that price should be recorded in the Secondary Rally column and should continue to be so recorded until a price had been made which exceeded the last figure recorded in the Natural Rally column. When that occurs, you should commence to record prices in the Natural Rally column once again.

(h) In case you have been recording in the Natural Rally column and a reaction should occur of approximately six points, but the price reached on that reaction was not lower than the last recorded figure in your Natural Reaction column that price should be entered in your Secondary Reaction column, and you should continue to record prices in that column until a price was made that was lower than the last price recorded in the Natural Reaction column. When that occurs, you should commence to record prices in the Natural Reaction column once again.

(Continued)

(7) The same rules apply when recording the Key Price—except that you use twelve points as a basis instead of six points used in individual stocks.

(8) The last price recorded in the Downward or Upward Trend columns becomes a Pivotal Point as soon as you begin to record prices in the Natural Rally or Natural Reaction columns. After a rally or reaction has ended you start to record again in the reverse column, and the extreme price made in the previous column then becomes another Pivotal Point. It is after two Pivotal Points have been reached that these records become of great value to you in helping you anticipate correctly the next movement of importance.

These Pivotal Points are drawn to your attention by having a double line drawn underneath them in either red [black and dashed] ink or black ink. Those lines are drawn for the express purpose of keeping those points before you, and should be watched very carefully whenever prices are made and recorded near or at one of those points. Your decision to act will then depend on how prices are recorded from then on.

(9) (a) When you see black lines drawn below the last recorded red-ink figure [black and boxed] in the Downward Trend column you may be given a signal to buy near that point.

(b) When black lines are drawn below a price recorded in the Natural Rally column, and if the stock on its next rally reaches a point near that Pivotal Point price, that is the time you are going to find out whether the market is strong enough definitely to change its course into the Upward Trend column.

(c) The reverse holds true when you see red [black and dashed] lines drawn under the last price recorded in the Upward Trend column, and when red [black and dashed] lines are drawn below the last price recorded in the Natural Reaction column.

(10) (a) This whole method is designed to enable one to see clearly whether a stock is acting the way it ought to, after its first Natural Rally or Reaction has occurred. If the movement is going to be resumed in a positive manner—either up or down—it will carry through its previous Pivotal Point—in individual stocks by three points or, in the Key Price by six points.

(b) If the stock fails to do this and in a reaction sells three points or more *below* the last Pivotal Point (recorded in the Upward Trend column with red [black and dashed] lines drawn underneath), it would indicate that the Upward Trend in the stock is over.

(c) Applying the rule to the Downward Trend: Whenever, after a Natural Rally has ended, new prices are being recorded in the Downward Trend column, these new prices must extend three or more points *below* the last Pivotal Point (with black lines underneath), if the Downward Trend is to be positively resumed.

(d) If the stock fails to do this, and on a rally sells three or more points *above* the last Pivotal Point (recorded in the Downward Trend column with black lines drawn underneath), it would indicate that the Downward Trend in the stock is over.

(e) When recording in the Natural Rally column, if the rally ends a short distance below the last Pivotal Point in the Upward Trend column (with red [black and dashed] lines underneath), and the stock reacts three or more points from that price, it is a danger signal, which would indicate the Upward Trend in that stock is over.

(f) When recording in the Natural Reaction column, if the reaction ends a short distance above the last Pivotal Point in the Downward Trend column (with black lines underneath), and the stock rallies three or more points from that price, it is a danger signal, which would indicate the Downward Trend in that stock is over.

On the following pages, on the lefthand side, are Jesse Livermore's original notes for his secret market key.

On **April 2nd** prices began to be recorded in Natural Rally column. Refer to Explanatory Rule 6-B. Draw black line under last price in Downward Trend column. Refer to Explanatory Rule 4-C.

On **April 28th**, prices began to be recorded in Natural Reaction column. Refer to Explanatory Rule 4-D.

CHART ONE

	SECONDARY RALLY	NATURAL RALLY	UPWARD TREND	DOWNWARD TREND	NATURAL REACTION	SECONDARY REACTION	SECONDARY RALLY	NATURAL RALLY	UPWARD TREND	DOWNWARD TREND	NATURAL REACTION	SECONDARY REACTION	SECONDARY RALLY	NATURAL RALLY	UPWARD TREND	DOWNWARD TREND	NATURAL REACTION	SECONDARY REACTION
		65¾																
				48½					57		43¼				122¾	91¾		
		62⅛							65⅞						128			
				48¼							50⅛						98⅜	
1938								56⅞										
DATE			U.S. STEEL						BETHLEHEM STEEL						KEY PRICE			
MAR. 23				47								50¼					97¼	
24																		
25				44¾						46¾						91½		
SAT. 26				44						46						90		
28				43⅝												89⅝		
29				39⅝						43						82⅝		
30				39						42⅛						81⅛		
31				38						40						78		
APR. 1																		
→ SAT. 2		43½						46⅜						89⅞				
4																		
5																		
6																		
7																		
8																		
SAT. 9		46½						49¾						96¼				
11																		
12																		
13		47¼												97				
14		47½												97¼				
SAT. 16		49						52						101				
18																		
19																		
20																		
21																		
22																		
SAT. 23																		
25																		
26																		
27																		
→ 28					43													
29					42⅜						45						87⅜	
SAT. 30																		
MAY 2					41½						44¼						85¾	
3																		
4																		

All of these prices recorded are brought forth from the preceding page in order to keep the Pivotal Points always before you.

During the period from **May 5th** to **May 21st** inclusive, no prices were recorded because no prices were made lower than the last price recorded in the Natural Reaction column. Nor was there sufficient rally to be recorded.

On **May 27th**, the price of Bethlehem Steel was recorded in red [black and boxed] because it was a lower price than the previous price recorded in the Downward Trend column. Refer to Explanatory Rule 6-C.

On **June 2nd**, Bethlehem Steel became a buy at 43. Refer to Explanatory Rule 10-C and D. On the same day U.S. Steel became a buy at 42¼. Refer to Explanatory Rule 10-F.

On **June 10th**, a price was recorded in the Secondary Rally column of Bethlehem Steel. Refer to Explanatory Rule 6-E.

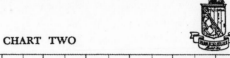

DATE	SECONDARY RALLY	NATURAL RALLY	UPWARD TREND	DOWNWARD TREND	NATURAL REACTION	SECONDARY REACTION	SECONDARY RALLY	NATURAL RALLY	UPWARD TREND	DOWNWARD TREND	NATURAL REACTION	SECONDARY REACTION	SECONDARY RALLY	NATURAL RALLY	UPWARD TREND	DOWNWARD TREND	NATURAL REACTION	SECONDARY REACTION
		49		[38]				52		[40]				101		[78]		
1938					$41\frac{1}{2}$						$44\frac{1}{4}$						$85\frac{3}{4}$	
DATE			U.S. STEEL						BETHLEHEM STEEL						KEY PRICE			
MAY 5																		
6																		
SAT. 7																		
9																		
10																		
11																		
12																		
13																		
SAT. 14																		
16																		
17																		
18																		
19																		
20																		
SAT. 21																		
23											$44\frac{1}{8}$						$85\frac{5}{8}$	
24											$43\frac{1}{2}$						85	
25				$41\frac{3}{8}$							$42\frac{1}{2}$						$83\frac{7}{8}$	
26				$40\frac{3}{8}$							$40\frac{1}{2}$						$80\frac{5}{8}$	
27				$39\frac{7}{8}$						[$39\frac{1}{4}$]							$79\frac{5}{8}$	
SAT. 28																		
31				$39\frac{1}{4}$													79	
JUNE 1																		
2																		
3																		
SAT. 4																		
6																		
7																		
8																		
9																		
10					$46\frac{1}{2}$													
SAT. 11																		
13																		
14																		
15																		
16																		

On **June 20th**, the price of U.S. Steel was recorded in the Secondary Rally column. Refer to Explanatory Rule 6-G.

On **June 24th**, prices of U.S. Steel and Bethlehem Steel were recorded in black ink [and circled] in the Upward Trend column. Refer to Explanatory Rule 5-A.

On **July 11th**, prices of U.S. Steel and Bethlehem Steel were recorded in the Natural Reaction column. Refer to Explanatory Rules 6-A and 4-A.

On **July 19th**, prices of U.S. Steel and Bethlehem Steel were recorded in the Upward Trend column in black ink [and circled] because those prices were higher than the last prices that were recorded in those columns. Refer to Explanatory Rule 4-B.

CHART THREE

	SECONDARY RALLY	NATURAL RALLY	UPWARD TREND	DOWNWARD TREND	NATURAL REACTION	SECONDARY REACTION	SECONDARY RALLY	NATURAL RALLY	UPWARD TREND	DOWNWARD TREND	NATURAL REACTION	SECONDARY REACTION	SECONDARY RALLY	NATURAL RALLY	UPWARD TREND	DOWNWARD TREND	NATURAL REACTION	SECONDARY REACTION
				38						40						78		
		49						52						101				
					39¼					39¾							79	
1938							46½											
DATE			U.S. STEEL						BETHLEHEM STEEL						KEY PRICE			
JUNE 17																		
SAT. 18																		
→ 20	45⅜						48¼						93⅝					
21	46½						49⅞						96⅜					
22	48½						50⅞						99⅜					
23		51¼						53¼						104½				
→ 24			53¾						55⅛						108⅞			
SAT. 25			54⅞						58⅛						113			
27																		
28																		
29			56⅞						60⅛						117			
30			58⅜						61⅝						120			
JULY 1			59												120⅝			
SAT. 2			60⅞						62½						123⅜			
5																		
6																		
7			61¾												124¼			
8																		
SAT. 9																		
→ 11					55⅝						56¾						112⅜	
12					55½												112¼	
13																		
14																		
15																		
SAT. 16																		
18																		
→ 19			62⅜						63⅛						125½			
20																		
21																		
22																		
SAT. 23																		
25			63¼												126⅜			
26																		
27																		
28																		
29																		

On **August 12th**, the price of U.S. Steel was recorded in the Secondary Reaction column because the price was not lower than the last price previously recorded in the Natural Reaction column. On the same day the price of Bethlehem Steel was recorded in the Natural Reaction column because that price was lower than the last price previously recorded in the Natural Reaction column.

On **August 24th**, prices of U.S. Steel and Bethlehem Steel were recorded in the Natural Rally column. Refer to Explanatory Rule 6-D.

On **August 29th**, prices of U.S. Steel and Bethlehem Steel were recorded in the Secondary Reaction column. Refer to Explanatory Rule 6-H.

DATE	SECONDARY RALLY	NATURAL RALLY	UPWARD TREND	DOWNWARD TREND	NATURAL REACTION	SECONDARY REACTION	SECONDARY RALLY	NATURAL RALLY	UPWARD TREND	DOWNWARD TREND	NATURAL REACTION	SECONDARY REACTION	SECONDARY RALLY	NATURAL RALLY	UPWARD TREND	DOWNWARD TREND	NATURAL REACTION	SECONDARY REACTION
			$61\frac{3}{4}$						$62\frac{1}{4}$						$124\frac{1}{4}$			
				$55\frac{1}{2}$						$56\frac{3}{4}$							$112\frac{1}{4}$	
			$63\frac{1}{4}$						$63\frac{3}{8}$						$126\frac{3}{8}$			
1938			U.S. STEEL						BETHLEHEM STEEL						KEY PRICE			
SAT. JULY 30																		
AUG. 1																		
2																		
3																		
4																		
5																		
SAT 6																		
8																		
9																		
10																		
11																		
→ 12					$56\frac{5}{8}$						$54\frac{7}{8}$						$111\frac{1}{2}$	
SAT 13					$56\frac{1}{2}$						$54\frac{5}{8}$						$111\frac{1}{8}$	
15																		
16																		
17																		
18																		
19																		
SAT 20																		
22																		
23																		
→ 24		$61\frac{5}{8}$						$61\frac{3}{8}$						123				
25																		
26		$61\frac{7}{8}$						$61\frac{1}{2}$						$123\frac{3}{8}$				
SAT 27																		
→ 29					$56\frac{1}{8}$						55						—	
30																		
31																		
SEPT 1																		
2																		
SAT 3																		
6																		
7																		
8																		
9																		
SAT 10																		

On **September 14th**, the price of U.S. Steel was recorded in the Downward Trend column. Refer to Explanatory Rule 5-B. On the same day a price was recorded in the Natural Reaction column of Bethlehem Steel. That price was still being recorded in the Natural Reaction column because it had not reached a price that was 3 points lower than its previous price with red [black and dashed] lines drawn. On September 20th, prices of U.S. Steel and Bethlehem Steel were recorded in the Natural Rally column. Refer to Explanatory Rule 6-C for U.S. Steel and 6-D for Bethlehem Steel.

On **September 24th**, the price of U.S. Steel was recorded in the Downward Trend column in red ink [black and boxed], being a new price in that column.

On **September 29th**, prices of U.S. Steel and Bethlehem Steel were recorded in the Secondary Rally column. Refer to Explanatory Rule 6-G.

On **October 5th**, the price of U.S. Steel was recorded in the Upward Trend column in black ink [and circled]. Refer to Explanatory Rule 5-A.

On **October 8th**, the price of Bethlehem Steel was recorded in the Upward Trend column in black ink [and circled]. Refer to Explanatory Rule 6-D.

CHART FIVE

	SECONDARY RALLY	NATURAL RALLY	UPWARD TREND	DOWNWARD TREND	NATURAL REACTION	SECONDARY REACTION	SECONDARY RALLY	NATURAL RALLY	UPWARD TREND	DOWNWARD TREND	NATURAL REACTION	SECONDARY REACTION	SECONDARY RALLY	NATURAL RALLY	UPWARD TREND	DOWNWARD TREND	NATURAL REACTION	SECONDARY REACTION
			63¼						63⅛						126⅝			
					55½						54⅜						111⅛	
								61½						123⅜				
		61⅞																
1938						56⅛						55						
DATE			U.S. STEEL						BETHLEHEM STEEL						KEY PRICE			
SEPT. 12																		
13					54¼						53⅝						107⅞	
→ 14				52							52½					104½		
15																		
16																		
SAT. 17																		
19																		
20		57⅝						58¼										
21		58												116¼				
22																		
23																		
→ SAT. 24				51⅞							52					103⅞		
26				51⅛							51¼					102⅜		
27																		
28				50⅞							51					101⅞		
→ 29	57⅛						57¾						114⅞					
30		59¼						59½						118¾				
SAT. OCT. 1		60¼						60						120¼				
3		60⅜						60⅜						120¾				
4																		
→ 5			62					62							124			
6			63					63							126			
7																		
→ SAT. 8			64¼						64						128¼			
10																		
11																		
13			65⅜						65⅛						130½			
14																		
SAT. 15																		
17																		
18																		
19																		
20																		
21																		
SAT. 22			65⅞						67½						133⅜			
24			66												133½			

On **November 18th**, prices of U.S. Steel and Bethlehem Steel were recorded in the Natural Reaction column. Refer to Explanatory Rule 6-A.

CHART SIX

	SECONDARY RALLY	NATURAL RALLY	UPWARD TREND	DOWNWARD TREND	NATURAL REACTION	SECONDARY REACTION	SECONDARY RALLY	NATURAL RALLY	UPWARD TREND	DOWNWARD TREND	NATURAL REACTION	SECONDARY REACTION	SECONDARY RALLY	NATURAL RALLY	UPWARD TREND	DOWNWARD TREND	NATURAL REACTION	SECONDARY REACTION
1938			66						67½						133½			
DATE			U.S. STEEL						BETHLEHEM STEEL						KEY PRICE			
OCT.25			66⅛						67⅞						134			
26																		
27			66½						68⅞						135⅜			
28																		
SAT.29																		
31																		
NOV.1									69						135½			
2																		
3									69½						136			
4																		
SAT.5																		
7			66¾						71⅞						138⅝			
9			69½						75⅜						144⅞			
10			70						75½						145½			
SAT.12			71¼						77⅝						148⅞			
14																		
15																		
16																		
17																		
→ 18					65⅛						71⅞						137	
SAT.19																		
21																		
22																		
23																		
25																		
SAT.26					63¼						71½						134¾	
28					61						68¾						129¾	
29																		
30																		
DEC.1																		
2																		
SAT.3																		
5																		
6																		
7																		
8																		

On **December 14th**, prices of U.S. Steel and Bethlehem Steel were recorded in the Natural Rally column. Refer to Explanatory Rule 6-D.

On **December 28th**, the price of Bethlehem Steel was recorded in the Upward Trend column in black ink [and circled], being a price higher than the last price previously recorded in that column.

On **January 4th**, the next trend of the market was being indicated according to the Livermore method. Refer to Explanatory Rules 10-A and B.

On **January 12th**, prices of U.S. Steel and Bethlehem Steel were recorded in the Secondary Reaction column. Refer to Explanatory Rule 6-H.

190

DATE	SECONDARY RALLY	NATURAL RALLY	UPWARD TREND	DOWNWARD TREND	NATURAL REACTION	SECONDARY REACTION	SECONDARY RALLY	NATURAL RALLY	UPWARD TREND	DOWNWARD TREND	NATURAL REACTION	SECONDARY REACTION	SECONDARY RALLY	NATURAL RALLY	UPWARD TREND	DOWNWARD TREND	NATURAL REACTION	SECONDARY REACTION
			$71\frac{1}{4}$ (circled)						$77\frac{5}{8}$ (circled)						$148\frac{7}{8}$ (circled)			
					61						$68\frac{3}{4}$						$129\frac{3}{4}$	
1938		U.S. STEEL						BETHLEHEM STEEL						KEY PRICE				
DEC.9																		
SAT.10																		
12																		
13																		
14		$66\frac{5}{8}$						$75\frac{1}{4}$						$141\frac{7}{8}$				
15		$67\frac{7}{8}$						$76\frac{3}{4}$						$143\frac{1}{2}$				
16																		
SAT.17																		
19																		
20																		
21																		
22																		
23																		
SAT.24																		
27																		
28		$67\frac{3}{4}$							78 (circled)						$145\frac{3}{4}$			
29																		
30																		
SAT.31 1939																		
JAN.3																		
4		70							80 (circled)							150 (circled)		
5																		
6																		
SAT.7																		
9																		
10																		
11								$73\frac{3}{4}$										
12				$62\frac{5}{8}$						$71\frac{1}{2}$							$139\frac{1}{8}$	
13																		
SAT.14																		
16																		
17																		
18																		
19																		
20																		
SAT.21				62						$69\frac{1}{2}$							$131\frac{1}{2}$	

On **January 23rd**, prices of U.S. Steel and Bethlehem Steel were recorded in the Downward Trend column. Refer to Explanatory Rule 5-B.

On **January 31st**, prices of U.S. Steel and Bethlehem Steel were recorded in the Natural Rally column. Refer to Explanatory Rules 6-C and 4-C.

CHART EIGHT

	SECONDARY RALLY	NATURAL RALLY	UPWARD TREND	DOWNWARD TREND	NATURAL REACTION	SECONDARY REACTION	SECONDARY RALLY	NATURAL RALLY	UPWARD TREND	DOWNWARD TREND	NATURAL REACTION	SECONDARY REACTION	SECONDARY RALLY	NATURAL RALLY	UPWARD TREND	DOWNWARD TREND	NATURAL REACTION	SECONDARY REACTION
			71 1/4						77 5/8						148 7/8			
					61						68 3/4						129 3/4	
		70							80						150			
1939						62						69 1/2						131 1/2
DATE			U.S. STEEL						BETHLEHEM STEEL						KEY PRICE			
JAN. 23				57 7/8						63 3/4						121 5/8		
24				56 1/2						63 1/4						119 3/4		
25				55 3/8						63						118 3/8		
26				53 1/4						60 1/4						113 1/2		
27																		
SAT. 28																		
30																		
31		59 1/2						68 1/2						128				
FEB. 1																		
2		60												128 1/2				
3																		
SAT. 4		60 5/8						69						129 5/8				
6								69 7/8						130 3/4				
7																		
8																		
9																		
10																		
SAT. 11																		
14																		
15																		
16								70 3/4						131 5/8				
17		61 1/8						71 1/4						132 3/8				
SAT. 18		61 1/4												132 1/2				
20																		
21																		
23																		
24		62 1/4						72 3/8						134 5/8				
SAT. 25		63 3/4						74 3/4						138 1/2				
27																		
28		64 3/4						75						139 3/4				
MAR. 1																		
2																		
3		64 7/8						75 1/4						140				
SAT. 4								75 1/2						140 3/8				
6																		
7																		

On **March 16th**, prices of U.S. Steel and Bethlehem Steel were recorded in the Natural Reaction column. Refer to Explanatory Rule 6-B.

On **March 30th**, the price of U.S. Steel was recorded in the Downward Trend column, being a lower price than was previously recorded in the Downward Trend column.

On **March 31st**, the price of Bethlehem Steel was recorded in the Downward Trend column, being a lower price than was previously recorded in the Downward Trend column.

On **April 15th**, prices of U.S. Steel and Bethlehem Steel were recorded in the Natural Rally column. Refer to Explanatory Rule 6-C.

	Secondary Rally	Natural Rally	Upward Trend	Downward Trend	Natural Reaction	Secondary Reaction	Secondary Rally	Natural Rally	Upward Trend	Downward Trend	Natural Reaction	Secondary Reaction	Secondary Rally	Natural Rally	Upward Trend	Downward Trend	Natural Reaction	Secondary Reaction
				$53\frac{1}{4}$						$60\frac{1}{4}$						$113\frac{1}{2}$		
1939	$64\frac{7}{8}$							$75\frac{1}{2}$						$140\frac{3}{8}$				
DATE			U.S. STEEL						BETHLEHEM STEEL						KEY PRICE			
MAR.8	65													$140\frac{1}{2}$				
9	$65\frac{1}{2}$							$75\frac{7}{8}$						$141\frac{3}{8}$				
10																		
SAT.11																		
13																		
14																		
15																		
16				$59\frac{5}{8}$						$69\frac{1}{4}$						$128\frac{7}{8}$		
17				$56\frac{3}{4}$						$66\frac{3}{4}$						$123\frac{1}{2}$		
SAT.18				$54\frac{3}{4}$						65						$119\frac{3}{4}$		
20																		
21																		
22				$53\frac{1}{2}$						$63\frac{5}{8}$						$117\frac{7}{8}$		
23																		
24																		
SAT.25																		
27																		
28																		
29																		
30				$52\frac{7}{8}$					62							$114\frac{7}{8}$		
31				$49\frac{7}{8}$						$58\frac{3}{4}$						$108\frac{5}{8}$		
APR. SAT.1																		
3																		
4				$48\frac{1}{4}$						$57\frac{5}{8}$						$105\frac{7}{8}$		
5																		
6				$47\frac{1}{4}$						$55\frac{1}{2}$						$102\frac{3}{4}$		
SAT.8				$44\frac{7}{8}$						$52\frac{1}{2}$						$97\frac{3}{8}$		
10																		
11				$44\frac{3}{4}$						$51\frac{5}{8}$						96		
12																		
13																		
14																		
SAT.15	50							$58\frac{1}{2}$						$108\frac{1}{2}$				
17																		
18																		
19																		

On **May 17th**, prices of U.S. Steel and Bethlehem Steel were recorded in the Natural Reaction column, and the next day, May 18th, the price of U.S. Steel was recorded in the Downward Trend column. Refer to Explanatory Rule 6-D. The next day, May 19th, a black line was drawn under the Downward Trend column in Bethlehem Steel, meaning a price was made that was the same as the last price recorded in the Downward Trend column.

On **May 25th**, prices of U.S. Steel and Bethlehem Steel were recorded in the Secondary Rally column. Refer to Explanatory Rule 6-C.

CHART TEN

	SECONDARY RALLY	NATURAL RALLY	UPWARD TREND	DOWNWARD TREND	NATURAL REACTION	SECONDARY REACTION	SECONDARY RALLY	NATURAL RALLY	UPWARD TREND	DOWNWARD TREND	NATURAL REACTION	SECONDARY REACTION	SECONDARY RALLY	NATURAL RALLY	UPWARD TREND	DOWNWARD TREND	NATURAL REACTION	SECONDARY REACTION
				44¾						51⅝						96		
1939		50						58½						108½				
DATE			U.S. STEEL						BETHLEHEM STEEL						KEY PRICE			
APR 20																		
21																		
SAT. 22																		
24																		
25																		
26																		
27																		
28																		
SAT. 29																		
MAY 1																		
2																		
3																		
4																		
5																		
SAT. 6																		
8																		
9																		
10																		
11																		
12																		
SAT. 13																		
15																		
16																		
→ 17					44⅝						52						96⅝	
18				43¼												95¼		
19																94⅞		
SAT. 20																		
22																		
23																		
24																		
→ 25	48¾						57¾						106½					
26	49						58						107					
SAT. 27	49⅜							—					107⅞					
29		50¼						59⅜						109⅝				
31		50⅞						60						110⅞				
JUNE 1																		

On **June 16th**, the price of Bethlehem Steel was recorded in the Natural Reaction column. Refer to Explanatory Rule 6-B.

On **June 28th**, the price of U.S. Steel was recorded in the Natural Reaction column. Refer to Explanatory Rule 6-B.

On **June 29th**, the price of Bethlehem Steel was recorded in the Downward Trend column, being a price lower than the last price recorded in the Downward Trend column.

On **July 13th**, prices of U.S. Steel and Bethlehem Steel were recorded in the Secondary Rally column. Refer to Explanatory Rule 6-G.

DATE	SECONDARY RALLY	NATURAL RALLY	UPWARD TREND	DOWNWARD TREND	NATURAL REACTION	SECONDARY REACTION	SECONDARY RALLY	NATURAL RALLY	UPWARD TREND	DOWNWARD TREND	NATURAL REACTION	SECONDARY REACTION	SECONDARY RALLY	NATURAL RALLY	UPWARD TREND	DOWNWARD TREND	NATURAL REACTION	SECONDARY REACTION
				$44\frac{3}{8}$						51						96		
		50						$58\frac{1}{2}$						$108\frac{1}{2}$				
				$43\frac{1}{4}$						—						$94\frac{7}{8}$		
1939		$50\frac{7}{8}$						60						$108\frac{7}{8}$				
DATE			U.S. STEEL					BETHLEHEM STEEL						KEY PRICE				
JUNE 2																		
SAT. 3																		
5																		
6																		
7																		
8																		
9																		
SAT. 10																		
12																		
13																		
14																		
15																		
→ 16								54										
SAT. 17																		
19																		
20																		
21																		
22																		
23																		
SAT. 24																		
26																		
27																		
→ 28					45						$52\frac{1}{2}$							$97\frac{1}{2}$	
→ 29				$43\frac{3}{4}$						51						$94\frac{3}{4}$		
30				$43\frac{5}{8}$						$50\frac{1}{4}$						$93\frac{7}{8}$		
SAT JULY 1																		
3																		
5																		
6																		
7																		
SAT. 8																		
10																		
11																		
12																		
→ 13	$48\frac{1}{4}$						$57\frac{1}{4}$						$105\frac{1}{2}$					
14																		

On **July 21st**, the price of Bethlehem Steel was recorded in the Upward Trend column, and the next day, July 22nd, the price of U.S. Steel was recorded in the Upward Trend column. Refer to Explanatory Rule 5-A.

On **August 4th**, prices of U.S. Steel and Bethlehem Steel were recorded in the Natural Reaction column. Refer to Explanatory Rule 4-A.

On **August 23rd**, the price of U.S. Steel was recorded in the Downward Trend column, being lower than the price previously recorded in the Downward Trend column.

200

CHART TWELVE

	U.S. STEEL						BETHLEHEM STEEL						KEY PRICE					
DATE	SECONDARY RALLY	NATURAL RALLY	UPWARD TREND	DOWNWARD TREND	NATURAL REACTION	SECONDARY REACTION	SECONDARY RALLY	NATURAL RALLY	UPWARD TREND	DOWNWARD TREND	NATURAL REACTION	SECONDARY REACTION	SECONDARY RALLY	NATURAL RALLY	UPWARD TREND	DOWNWARD TREND	NATURAL REACTION	SECONDARY REACTION
				43¼						51⅝						94⅞		
		50⅞						60						110⅞				
					43⅝					50¼						93⅞		
1939	48¼						57¼						105½					
SAT. JULY 15																		
17	50¾							60⅜						111⅛				
18		51⅞						62						113⅞				
19																		
20																		
→ 21		52½							63					115½				
SAT. 22			54⅛						65						119⅛			
24																		
25			55⅛						65¾						120⅞			
26																		
27																		
28																		
SAT. 29																		
31																		
AUG. 1																		
2																		
3																		
→ 4					49½						59½						109	
SAT. 5																		
7					49¼												108¾	
8																		
9											59						108¼	
10					47¾						58						105¾	
11					47												105	
SAT. 12																		
14																		
15																		
16																		
17					46½												104½	
18					45						55⅛						100⅛	
SAT. 19																		
21					43⅜						53⅜						96¾	
22																		
→ 23				42⅝													96	
24				41⅝							51⅞					93½		
25																		

On **August 29th**, prices of U.S. Steel and Bethlehem Steel were recorded in the Natural Rally column. Refer to Explanatory Rule 6-D.

On **September 2nd**, prices of U.S. Steel and Bethlehem Steel were recorded in the Upward Trend column, being higher prices than the last prices previously recorded in the Upward Trend column.

On **September 14th**, prices of U.S. Steel and Bethlehem Steel were recorded in the Natural Reaction column. Refer to Explanatory Rules 6-A and 4-A.

On **September 19th**, prices of U.S. Steel and Bethlehem Steel were recorded in the Natural Rally column. Refer to Explanatory Rules 6-D and 4-B.

On **September 28th**, prices for U.S. Steel and Bethlehem Steel were recorded in the Secondary Reaction column. Refer to Explanatory Rule 6-H.

On **October 6th**, prices of U.S. Steel and Bethlehem Steel were recorded in the Secondary Rally column. Refer to Explanatory Rule 6-G.

202

Date	Secondary Rally	Natural Rally	Upward Trend	Downward Trend	Natural Reaction	Secondary Reaction	Secondary Rally	Natural Rally	Upward Trend	Downward Trend	Natural Reaction	Secondary Reaction	Secondary Rally	Natural Rally	Upward Trend	Downward Trend	Natural Reaction	Secondary Reaction
	U.S. STEEL						BETHLEHEM STEEL						KEY PRICE					
				$43\frac{3}{8}$						$50\frac{1}{4}$						$93\frac{7}{8}$		
			$55\frac{7}{8}$						$65\frac{3}{4}$						$120\frac{7}{8}$			
1939				$41\frac{5}{8}$							$51\frac{7}{8}$						$93\frac{1}{2}$	
SAT. AUG 26																		
28																		
→ 29		48						$60\frac{1}{2}$						$108\frac{1}{2}$				
30																		
31																		
SEPT. 1		52						$65\frac{1}{4}$						$117\frac{1}{2}$				
→ SAT. 2			$55\frac{1}{4}$						$70\frac{3}{4}$						$125\frac{5}{8}$			
5			$66\frac{1}{8}$						$85\frac{1}{2}$						$152\frac{5}{8}$			
6																		
7																		
8			$69\frac{3}{4}$						87						$156\frac{3}{4}$			
SAT. 9			70						$88\frac{3}{4}$						$158\frac{1}{4}$			
11			$78\frac{5}{8}$						100						$178\frac{5}{8}$			
12			$82\frac{1}{4}$												$182\frac{1}{4}$			
13																		
→ 14				$76\frac{3}{8}$						$91\frac{3}{4}$						$168\frac{1}{8}$		
15																		
SAT. 16				$75\frac{1}{2}$						$88\frac{3}{8}$						$163\frac{7}{8}$		
18				$70\frac{1}{2}$						$83\frac{3}{4}$						$154\frac{1}{4}$		
→ 19		78						$92\frac{3}{8}$						$170\frac{3}{8}$				
20		$80\frac{5}{8}$						$95\frac{5}{8}$						$176\frac{1}{4}$				
21																		
22																		
SAT. 23																		
25																		
26																		
27																		
→ 28				$75\frac{5}{8}$							89						$168\frac{1}{8}$	
29				$73\frac{1}{2}$							$86\frac{3}{4}$						$160\frac{1}{4}$	
SAT. 30																		
OCT. 2																		
3																		
4				73							$86\frac{1}{4}$						$159\frac{1}{4}$	
5																		
→ 6	$78\frac{1}{2}$							$92\frac{3}{4}$						$171\frac{1}{4}$				
SAT. 7																		

On **November 3rd**, the price of U.S. Steel was recorded in the Secondary Reaction column, being a price lower than the last previous price recorded in that column.

On **November 9th**, a dash was made in the Natural Reaction column of U.S. Steel, being the same price that was last recorded in the Natural Reaction column, and on the same day a new price was recorded in the Natural Reaction column of Bethlehem Steel, being a lower price than the last price previously recorded in that column.

CHART FOURTEEN

DATE	SECONDARY RALLY	NATURAL RALLY	UPWARD TREND	DOWNWARD TREND	NATURAL REACTION	SECONDARY REACTION	SECONDARY RALLY	NATURAL RALLY	UPWARD TREND	DOWNWARD TREND	NATURAL REACTION	SECONDARY REACTION	SECONDARY RALLY	NATURAL RALLY	UPWARD TREND	DOWNWARD TREND	NATURAL REACTION	SECONDARY REACTION
			(82¾)						(100)						(182¾)			
				70½						83¾						159¼		
		80⅝						95⅝						176¼				
					73						86¼						159¼	
1939	78½						92¾						171¼					
DATE		*U.S. STEEL*						*BETHLEHEM STEEL*						*KEY PRICE*				
OCT.9																		
10																		
11																		
13																		
SAT.14																		
16																		
17	78⅞						93⅞						172¾					
18	79¼												173½					
19																		
20																		
SAT.21																		
23																		
24																		
25																		
26																		
27																		
SAT.28																		
30																		
31																		
NOV.1																		
2																		
→ 3					72½													
SAT.4																		
6																		
8					72⅛							86⅛						158¼	
→ 9				—							83¼						153¾		
10				68¾							81¾						150½		
13																		
14																		
15																		
16																		
17																		
SAT.18																		
20																		
21																		
22																		

On **November 24th**, the price of U.S. Steel was recorded in the Downward Trend column. Refer to Explanatory Rule 6-E, and the next day, November 25th, the price of Bethlehem Steel was recorded in the Downward Trend column. Refer to Explanatory Rule 6-E.

On **December 7th**, the prices of U.S. Steel and Bethlehem Steel were recorded in the Natural Rally column. Refer to Explanatory Rule 6-C.

DATE	SECONDARY RALLY	NATURAL RALLY	UPWARD TREND	DOWNWARD TREND	NATURAL REACTION	SECONDARY REACTION	SECONDARY RALLY	NATURAL RALLY	UPWARD TREND	DOWNWARD TREND	NATURAL REACTION	SECONDARY REACTION	SECONDARY RALLY	NATURAL RALLY	UPWARD TREND	DOWNWARD TREND	NATURAL REACTION	SECONDARY REACTION
			(82 3/4)						(100)						(182 3/4)			
				70 1/2							83 3/4						154 1/4	
		80 5/8						95 5/8						176 1/4				
1939					68 3/4						81 1/4						150 1/2	
			U.S. STEEL						BETHLEHEM STEEL						KEY PRICE			
NOV.24				66 7/8							81					147 7/8		
SAT.25										80 3/8						147 7/8		
27																		
28																		
29				65 7/8						78 1/8						144		
30				63 3/8						77						140 5/8		
DEC.1																		
SAT.2																		
4																		
5																		
6																		
7		69 3/4						84						153 3/4				
8																		
SAT.9																		
11																		
12																		
13																		
14								84 3/8						154 5/8				
15																		
SAT.16																		
18																		
19																		
20																		
21																		
22																		
SAT.23																		
26																		
27																		
28																		
29																		
SAT.30																		
1940 JAN.2																		
3																		
4																		
5																		
SAT.6																		

On **January 9th**, prices of U.S. Steel and Bethlehem Steel were recorded in the Natural Reaction column. Refer to Explanatory Rule 6-B.

On **January 11th**, prices of U.S. Steel and Bethlehem Steel were recorded in the Downward Trend column, being lower than the last recorded prices in the Downward Trend columns.

On **February 7th**, prices are recorded in the Natural Rally column of Bethlehem Steel, this being the first day it rallied the required distance of six points. The following day U.S. Steel is recorded in addition to Bethlehem Steel and the Key Price, the latter having rallied the proper distance to be used in recording.

CHART SIXTEEN

	SECONDARY RALLY	NATURAL RALLY	UPWARD TREND	DOWNWARD TREND	NATURAL REACTION	SECONDARY REACTION	SECONDARY RALLY	NATURAL RALLY	UPWARD TREND	DOWNWARD TREND	NATURAL REACTION	SECONDARY REACTION	SECONDARY RALLY	NATURAL RALLY	UPWARD TREND	DOWNWARD TREND	NATURAL REACTION	SECONDARY REACTION
				63 5/8						77						140 5/8		
1940		69 3/4						84 7/8						154 5/8				
			U.S. STEEL						BETHLEHEM STEEL						KEY PRICE			
JAN. 8																		
→ 9					64 1/4						78 1/2						142 3/4	
10					63 3/4												142 1/4	
→ 11				62						76 1/2						138 1/2		
12				60 1/8						74 1/8						134 1/4		
SAT. 13				59 5/8						73 1/2						133 1/8		
15				57 1/2						72						129 1/2		
16																		
17																		
18				56 7/8						71 1/2						128 3/8		
19										71						127 7/8		
SAT. 20																		
22				55 7/8						70 1/8						126		
23																		
24																		
25																		
26																		
SAT. 27																		
29																		
30																		
31																		
FEB. 1																		
2																		
SAT. 3																		
5																		
6																		
→ 7								76 3/8										
8		61						78						139				
9		61 3/4						79 1/2						141 1/4				
SAT. 10																		
13																		
14																		
15																		
16					56 1/8													
SAT. 17																		

About the Author

Richard Smitten is the author of numerous books including *Jesse Livermore: World's Greatest Stock Trader, The Godmother, Capital Crimes, Legal Tender, False Witness, Inside the Cocaine Cartel,* and *Death Stream.*

With the public company Stock Market Solutions (symbol SMKT on the Nasdaq Bulletin Board), Smitten currently is developing a fully automated software program that allows the trader to trade like Jesse Livermore.

Smitten is a full-time author and trader. He has recently completed a biography of Ernest Hemingway. He lives in the French Quarter, New Orleans, Louisiana.

Index